Renewable Energy Resources and Rural Applications in the Developing World

AAAS Selected Symposia Series

Published by Westview Press
5500 Central Avenue, Boulder, Colorado

for the

American Association for the Advancement of Science
1776 Massachusetts Ave., N.W., Washington, D.C.

Renewable Energy Resources and Rural Applications in the Developing World

Edited by Norman L. Brown

AAAS Selected Symposium 6

AAAS Selected Symposia Series

Published in 1978 in the United States of America by

    Westview Press, Inc.
    5500 Central Avenue
    Boulder, Colorado 80301
    Frederick A. Praeger, Publisher and Editorial Director

Library of Congress Number: 77-18549
ISBN: 0-89158-433-1

Printed and bound in the United States of America

About the Book

The energy situation in developing countries is desperate. Because these countries are primarily dependent on fossil fuels--chiefly oil--for industrial growth, they have been hard hit by oil price increases. Further, in the rural areas, where most of the population lives, there are limited supplies of increasingly expensive diesel fuel or kerosene. Noncommercial energy sources such as firewood, dung, and agricultural residues are generally used in rural areas, but under the pressure of growing populations the forests are disappearing. This is resulting in a critical shortage of firewood for cooking and heating, as well as in the destruction of the environment. In addition, when dung and agricultural residues are burned, valuable fertilizers are destroyed. Thus, the rural areas--the sources of food and fiber--face a particularly alarming situation.

Small-scale, decentralized technologies for exploiting the sun's energy, received directly or as wind, flowing water, or biomass, provide potential solutions to the problem of rural energy needs. These technologies have been the subject of numerous studies, including two by the National Academy of Sciences. In this volume, members of the two academy study panels have joined with other experts to discuss the status of these technologies and to place them in a realistic context.

Contents

List of Figures

Chapter 6

List of Tables

Foreword

The *AAAS Selected Symposia Series* was begun in 1977 to
provide a means for more permanently recording and more
widely disseminating some of the valuable material which is
discussed at the AAAS Annual National Meetings. The volumes
in this *Series* are based on symposia held at the Meetings
which address topics of current and continuing significance,
both within and among the sciences, and in the areas in which
science and technology impact on public policy. The *Series*
format is designed to provide for rapid dissemination of information, so the papers are not typeset but are reproduced
directly from the camera copy submitted by the authors, without copy editing. The papers are reviewed and edited by
the symposia organizers who then become the editors of the
various volumes. Most papers published in this *Series* are
original contributions which have not been previously published, although in some cases additional papers from other
sources have been added by an editor to provide a more comprehensive view of a particular topic. Symposia may be reports of new research or reviews of established work, particularly work of an interdisciplinary nature, since the AAAS
Annual Meeting typically embraces the full range of the
sciences and their societal implications.

WILLIAM D. CAREY
Executive Officer
American Association for
the Advancement of Science

About the Editor and Authors

Norman L. Brown is country program specialist with the Office of International Affiars at the Department of Energy. As such, he is chief technical adviser to DOE's program of energy development with less developed countries. His international interdisciplinary background in science and technology, particularly energy and food problems, has involved him in seeking and encouraging appropriate technological solutions. He was the staff study director for Energy for Rural Development *(National Academy of Sciences, 1976).*

Joseph J. Ermenc, professor of engineering at Dartmouth College, specializes in mechanical engineering and the history and philosophy of technology development. He is the author of an 8-volume series, Dartmough Readings on Technology, *and 38 volumes of interviews with outstanding innovators. He was a member of the NAS panel that contributed to* Energy for Rural Development *(NAS, 1976).*

Raymond C. Loehr, director of the Environmental Studies Program and professor of civil, environmental and agricultural engineering at Cornell University, has published over 100 technical papers and three books, including Agricultural Waste Management *(Academic Press, 1974) and* Land as a Waste Management Alternative, *which he edited. He is also an advisor to various governmental and private organizations.*

George O. G. Löf, director of the Solar Energy Applications Laboratory at Colorado State University and vice-president of the Solaron Corporation in Denver, is the author of over 100 books and papers on energy conservation, solar energy utilization, heat transfer, and environmental engineering. He is former president of the International Solar Energy Society and in 1976 received the Lyndon Baines Johnson Foundation award for contribution to the betterment of mankind. He too was a member of the NAS panel on Energy for Rural Development.

José M. Miccolis is special assistant to the president of the National Council for Scientific Development of Brazil in Rio de Janeiro, and director of the Brazilian Science Policy Project at George Washington University. He is the author of several publications concerning energy policy in Brazil.

John W. Powell, director of the Technology Consultancy Centre at the University of Science and Technology in Kumasi, Ghana, has conducted a six-year study of small industries in Ghana. He is the author and editor of two books in mechanical engineering.

Morton B. Prince is acting director for photovoltaics of the Division of Solar Energy at the Department of Energy. In 1954, he developed the Bell Solar Battery at the Bell Telephone Laboratories, and later developed commercial applications of the silicon photovoltaic cell at the Hoffman Electronics Corporation.

Roger Revelle is professor of science and public policy at the University of California, San Diego, and the Richard Saltonstall Professor of Population Policy at Harvard University. He is former president of the American Association for the Advancement of Science, a member of the National Academy of Sciences, and the recipient of numerous honorary degrees. His numerous publications in the areas of geophysics, national resource development, and population studies include Survival Equation: Man, Resources, and His Environment *(Houghton Mifflin, 1971) and* Population and Social Change *(Crane-Russak, 1972), both of which he coedited.*

Sharat K. Tewari, a scientist with the Wind Energy Group at the National Aeronautical Laboratory in Bangalore, India, is involved in analysis of wind energy as an alternative energy source, and hardware development in wind power. He has written several papers in this field.

Renewable Energy Resources and Rural Applications in the Developing World

Introduction

Norman L. Brown

The developing countries that are not fortunate
enough to be oil producers are faced with energy needs that
are growing more and more difficult to meet. Primarily
dependent on oil for industrial growth and agricultural development, they have been hard hit by oil price increases.
With little or no flexibility to meet these energy needs
with other energy resources and generally unable to compensate for increased oil prices by increasing their exports,
the less developed countries (LDCs) find themselves in a
progressively worsening position to compete for the limited
supplies of fossil fuel.

In most of these countries only a small proportion
of the population is served by a power distribution network.
The rural areas, where the majority of the LDC population
lives, generally depend on limited supplies of diesel fuel
or kerosene -- with more or less uncertain transport -- or
"noncommercial" energy sources such as firewood, dung, and
agricultural residues.

Thus, the LDCs have two distinct energy needs. On the
one hand, industrial growth is dependent on conventional
urban energy systems that use commercial energy sources and
technologies that are already in use or are being developed
in the industrialized countries. Agricultural development
schemes -- the "green revolution," for example -- pegged
to mechanization and manufactured nitrogenous fertilizers
also depend on these energy sources and technologies. On
the other hand, the majority of the population in most LDCs,
living in the rural areas, is isolated from central power
distribution. They would therefore particularly benefit
from development of technologies to exploit renewable energy
resources of the sun, wind, and flowing water.

Most of the energy-related assistance that has been provided the less developed countries to-date has focussed attention on urban/industrial-sector requirements. Only recently have development-assistance organizations focussed attention on the needs of the rural areas. This shift stems from a growing awareness of the importance of the way energy is gathered and used, and an increased understanding, on the part of the donor nations, of the necessity to focus on the needs of the rural populations of the less developed countries.

The choice of energy technology made by developing countries will have a long-term impact on their development that is more widespread and significant than that of any other technological choice currently facing them. Choosing conventional large-scale capital-intensive technologies implies a priori decisions, conscious or not, about many important policies. These include the course of urban development, expanding industrialization, environmental impact, large-scale borrowing (or foreign investment) with long-term indebtedness and problems of debt servicing, increased dependence on fossil fuels or commitment to nuclear energy, and last but not least, the foreign policy stance dictated by these requirements.

On the other hand, the choice of small-scale decentralized power systems (e.g., solar heating, cooling, and generation of electricity; windmills; small-scale hydroelectric plants) implies a different set of a priori decisions. These include, for example, de-emphasis of western-style industrialization as the sole or primary immediate goal of development; dispersal of industry and, perhaps, changes in financial mechanisms; and a shift from western agricultural techniques to emphasis on improvement of indigenous agricultural practices, with consequent reduced demand for energy-consuming nitrogenous fertilizers. All of these factors could contribute significantly to a slowing down of migration to the cities and urban growth, with important effects on the rate of growth of dependence on commercial energy supplies.

In making these choices, less developed countries must decide on the relative importance of the commercial-sector energy needs versus those of the traditional rural sector. Interest in small-scale technologies for exploiting energy received from the sun - whether directly or in the form of biomass, wind, or flowing water - has been increasing recently in both the industrialized and the developing world. In a recent report (1) the National Academy of Sciences examined these technologies in terms of their near- and long-term availability, particularly for use in rural areas of the less

developed countries. The report concluded that, for the most
part, these technologies will have little short-term effect
on energy-use patterns in urban areas. However, application
of these technologies to improving the quality - and productivity - of rural life may have significant long-term effects
on the trend toward urbanization.

It was the objective of the symposium from which this
collection of papers was drawn to examine these technologies
and their near-term applicability in the developing country
rural setting, and place them in a realistic economic context.*

A discussion of energy uses in developing countries by
Roger Revelle provides an appropriate introduction to the
symposium. An analysis of estimated per capita uses of energy in rural areas of seven developing countries shows dramatically the overwhelming portion that is devoted to domestic
activities and agriculture. Furthermore, the analysis demonstrates the importance of taking into account the noncommercial energy sources in developing countries. In two of the
countries examined, no commercial energy at all is available
in rural areas, and in four others, the ratio of noncommercial to commercial energy ranges from 6.3 to 157. Using
Nepal as an example, Professor Revelle points out the serious
environmental consequences of the incessant search, by rural
people, for the most common noncommercial fuel available to
them--firewood. The discussion serves as an illustration of
the need to make renewable energy resources available to
villagers in rural areas of developing countries in order to
make it possible for them to improve the quality of their
lives.

In a down-to-earth assessment of solar thermal technologies, George O. G. Löf contrasts the cost of converting
solar heat to mechanical and electrical energy, based on
current manufacturing costs in the United States, with conventional means of producing mechanical or electrical power.
The comparison is discouraging, and accounts for the slow
growth of the solar technology industry in the industrialized
countries. Nevertheless, this pessimism must be tempered
with a realization that in many developing countries, for
a variety of reasons - often simply transportation costs
and uncertainties, and maintenance problems - the cost of
generating electricity is much higher than in the U.S.

---

*The paper presented by Dr. Ibrahim Sakr, referred to in the
"Summary and Discussion" by Roger Revelle, was not available
for publication in this volume.

For example, the cost of producing electricity in Mauritania is over $1.00 per kilowatt hour. Thus, in such areas solar technologies not yet economically competitive in the United States would certainly be economically attractive. Most important, of course, are those technologies that could find immediate application, such as crop drying and distillation.

Morton Prince's discussion of the U.S. National Photovoltaic Program similarly describes the cost factors that are the main concern of development programs in the United States. The goal of this program is a cost reduction to US $.50 per peak watt by 1985, and there is reason to believe that this goal may be reached earlier. Although some of the cost reduction is expected to result from development of thin-film techniques and novel devices, the bulk is expected to come from automation techniques that reduce the amount of hand labor involved in fabrication of solar cells. The argument is made that "the market for photovoltaic systems is not sufficiently large to justify additional investment by private industry" to accelerate initiation of these cost-reduction procedures. It must be borne in mind, however, that this argument is made in the context of appraisal of the known domestic market and labor costs in the United States. The potential market in LDCs has yet to be ascertained; there are parts of the developing world where electricity costs from photovoltaics are almost competitive now with solar arrays at US $15 per peak watt.

Second, the history of the semiconductor industry has shown that labor-intensive fabrication can be economically performed in developing areas. Thus the medium-term prospects of the use of photovoltaic technology for generation of electricity in developing countries are not necessarily as dim as would be inferred from the description of the U.S. National Photovoltaic Program.

Brazil is currently engaged in a coherent, long-range program to make use of its vast resources to supply the increasing needs of its long-term development goals. With oil accounting for half the total commercial energy used, the government is emphasizing the development of alternative energy technologies. Jose Miccolis' paper details the current energy picture of Brazil and the multitude of schemes for conserving and supplementing scarce supplies that are being considered.

Solar energy is seen as playing an important role in Brazil's medium- and long-term plans, in view of Brazil's 8.5 million square kilometers lying almost entirely between the Equator and the Tropic of Capricorn. Development of solar thermal technologies has received substantial support, but institutional changes are seen as needed to accelerate this activity.

Bioconversion, however, is the subject of a major effort. The production of ethyl alcohol as a fuel for internal-combustion engines, by fermentation of sugar and cassava, is being substantially supported. Serious consideration is being given to the use of hydrocarbon-producing plants, as a way of converting sunlight, via photosynthesis, to valuable chemical feedstocks, and fermentation processes to produce fuel (methane) and valuable nutrients (vitamins, enzymes, amino acids) are included in biomass conversion plans.

Mr. Miccolis' description of the energy needs and resources of Brazil is illustrative of the problems facing a country that has recently "graduated" from most foreign assistance programs, but finds itself facing not only a rapidly developing industrial sector, but continued problems of rural development.

One of the earliest concerted programs of development of wind-energy conversion systems for use in rural areas of a developing country was started in India more than twenty years ago. However, S. K. Tewari points out that the "optimism of cheap electricity from the grids," based on the assumption of cheap and plentiful petroleum supplies, was responsible for halting the program in 1966. The oil price increase of 1973 triggered a new and more intense interest in renewable energy resources in India, and the wind-energy conversion program was resumed. In common with many other developing countries, India is primarily concerned with the use of windmills to provide shaft power for pumping water and grinding grain, replacing the muscle power of people and animals. Generation of electricity by windmill systems seems of secondary importance in the near term for several reasons. Although the high costs of transmission lines would seem to argue for decentralized electricity generation, statistics show that in the 20-30% of India's half-million villages that are electrified, the primary use of electricity is to operate irrigation pumpsets and grind grain, i.e., to provide shaft power. Electricity for lighting can be afforded only by the rich villagers. Thus, India's wind-energy conversion program is aimed primarily at providing mechanical power.

Mr. Tewari makes a point that is important in evaluating the use of all the so-called non-conventional energy technologies in developing countries. Conventional methods of cost/benefit analysis frequently fail to give adequate weight to the social benefits that result from making energy available where it had not been and would not be available for some time to come if conventional sources were relied on. The value of supplying irrigation water can be estimated in terms of increased crop production. But the long-term benefits in improvement of the quality of rural life are difficult to quantify and are easily glossed over in economic comparisons. The unique ability of solar technologies - heat, wind, biomass, hydropower - to provide power in isolated communities, without the necessity of building roads, providing transport, or constructing transmission lines - to say nothing of avoiding the burden of increasing costs and scarcity of petroleum-based fuels - must be given appropriate weight in national planning schemes.

The issue of using conventional economic analysis, developed for use in the industrialized countries, to evaluate energy technologies in rural areas of the developing world arises again in considering the potential of small-scale hydropower. In a detailed history of the development of water wheels and turbines, Joseph J. Ermenc describes the important role that these devices played in the development of rural areas in the industrialized world. He notes, however, that this technology was displaced by the advent of large-scale central thermal and hydropower stations, rural distribution of electricity, the internal combustion engine, and improved rural transportation. But all of these factors were - and are - based on the availability of cheap and plentiful petroleum. Although cheap and plentiful are relative terms, fossil fuels are obviously not cheap and plentiful in developing countries. With a realistic awareness of the implications of this situation in terms of such things as road building, transportation, transmission line construction, and materials, and manufacturing costs for large-scale power equipment, the exploitation of small-scale hydropower sites for decentralized power systems becomes well worth examining. In this, the People's Republic of China seems to be leading the way, with thousands of unites of less than 100-kW capacity installed in rural areas. It is encouraging to note that interest in this approach has been developing rapidly in the United States, both in commercial manufacture of small turbines and as part of the national development program of the new Department of Energy.

The deforestation of many parts of the world resulting from the incessant search for cooking fuel is an issue of world-wide concern. Nepal estimates, for example, that at current rates of removal and regrowth only 12 to 13 years of accessible forest are left in that country. For countries fortunate enough to have forests to support a substantial lumber industry, however, it behooves them to use their forest waste efficiently in order to maintain, or even improve, their present resources. Dr. John W. Powell describes Ghana's efforts to minimize the wood waste from its forests by a research and development program to utilize sawdust for cooking and to improve the efficiency of traditional methods of making charcoal. There is no doubt, however, that one of the most significant ways to reduce the denudation of forests for firewood is by improving the efficiency of traditional wood-burning cookstoves. With efficiencies of the order of 10 percent, even small improvements would significantly reduce the amount of firewood consumed - whether as wood or as charcoal.

Conversion of biomass into a particularly useful form of energy by anaerobic digestion is discussed by Raymond C. Loehr. In a lucid paper describing the state of the technology, the technical and institutional requirements, raw material needs, and advantages and disadvantages, Professor Loehr puts the process in a meaningful overall context. He points out that the use of alternative energy technologies in rural areas of developing countries should be aimed at reduction of human drudgery, minimum capital investment and operating expense, and production of energy in a form convenient for storage. In addition, where biomass conversion is concerned, agricultural productivity should be increased, the efficiency of the use of biomass (wood, cattle dung, crop residues) must be increased, and the use of plant fuels in general must be decreased to prevent deforestation and maintain soil tilth. The production of methane by anaerobic digestion of human, animal, and agricultural wastes comes close to meeting most of these goals by producing a combustible gas that can be stored and a stabilized residue that is a valuable fertilizer, in equipment that can be built and maintained on a village level.

The experience that has already been gained at the village level in countries such as Taiwan, India, Korea, and the People's Republic of China justifies optimism about the prospects of increasing the use of this process. Nevertheless, competent technical guidance and a careful evaluation of social and economic feasibility are needed in each situation.

Two things are apparent from the papers presented in this symposium and from the variety of developments reported in other forums. First, the developing countries themselves have begun to awaken to the implications of the commitment to fossil fuels and central-power station technologies, by

pressing for technologies that rely on renewable resources.
Second, the principal barrier to greater use of these technologies has been their high initial cost per unit output
and the almost universal access to the power distributions
systems associated with larger-scale alternatives in the
industrialized countries. The existence of these alternatives has inhibited the development and mass production of
small-scale devices that would simplify their design and
lower their cost. Without these alternatives, therefore,
the developing countries will constitute the major market
for small-scale decentralized power systems for the next
five to ten years.

Thus, it is encouraging to note that the U.S. Energy
Research and Development Administration, recently incorporated in the Department of Energy, has stated that it is
taking steps to "initiate research, development, demonstration, and related activities aimed at helping to meet the
energy needs of developing countries" in a program that
"will seek technological solutions appropriate to the
resources and the social, economic, and political goals of
the developing countries. By providing a vehicle for consideration of alternatives that combine exploitation of renewable energy resources with technologies of use on a
scale suited to rural community and single-family needs,
the activities work to achieve maximum benefit for both
the United States and developing countries." (2)

Furthermore, it is not merely a question of transferring technology to developing countries--all too often technology developed in the context of an industrialized society
is irrelevant, at best, or harmful, at worst, to developing
countries. What is needed, in the long run, are technologies
suited to the needs and constraints of the country where it
is to be used. And perhaps most important is the need to
develop technologies to help meet what Roger Revelle has referred to as our uniquely human needs. In a discussion of
technology transfer in another forum (3), Professor Revelle
noted that". . . we human beings have some uniquely human
needs, because of our special characteristics as human
beings. One of the ways in which we are special is that we
are able to remember the past and to think about the future.
We go beyond satisfying the veterinary needs [food, warmth,
shelter, sexual satisfaction, and health], and provide the
means for satisfying the uniquely human needs that depend
upon our character as time-binding animals. Four of these
needs are hope, security, participation, and remembrance.
Every human being must have hope, the hope that the future
will be better than the present. Every human being needs
some feeling of security, that the future won't be worse than

the present. Every human being needs a faith that he will
attain some kind of immortality or remembrance, that is,
soemthing that goes beyond his own short lifespan, not for-
ever, but for a while.

"Most poor people in most less-developed countries
satisfy these needs by having children; their hope for the
future lies in children; children are their security in
old age or sickness; children give them a sense of participation in the future; and they give them remembrance.
Unless we can satisfy these uniquely human needs in other
ways, the world is heading for a Malthusian catastrophe,
and the problems of technology transfer will disappear in
a grand Armageddon."

References

1. Energy for Rural Development - Renewable Resources and
   Alternative Technologies for Developing Countries.
   1976. Washington, D.C.: National Academy of Sciences.

2. U.S. Energy Research and Development Administration.
   1976. Policy statement issues by Robert C. Seamans,
   Jr., October 26.

3. Revelle, Roger R. 1976. Department of State. Edited
   transcript of November 17, 1976 Meeting, preparation
   for 1979 U.N. Conference on Science and Technology for
   Development. Washington, D.C.

1

Requirements for Energy in the Rural Areas of Developing Countries

Roger Revelle

There is a paradox of energy in the rural areas of developing countries. Both too little energy and too much energy are used, and the basic problems are to find ways to provide more energy and at the same time to conserve energy.

The economic chasm that divides the world separates two vastly different levels and kinds of energy use. More than 5/6 of all the energy obtained from fossil fuels and hydroelectric and nuclear power is used by the 12 hundred million inhabitants of the rich countries, and less than 1/6 by the nearly 3 billion inhabitants of the poor countries. Just the reverse is true of the traditional sources of energy: human and animal labor, firewood, crop residues and animal wastes. These were the predominant--indeed almost the only--sources of energy everywhere in the world until about 200 years ago. A man was actually hanged in England during the 15th century for burning coal.

The total quantities of energy obtained from traditional sources in the poor countries today are larger than their consumption of fossil fuels and they greatly exceed the uses in the rich countries. In the rural areas of the poor countries energy obtained from local, noncommercial sources by the people themselves is 5 to 10 times that obtained from commercial sources. Nevertheless, usable energy is in very short supply and the needs both for a large increase in supplies and for conservation--more efficient utilization--are great. From an energy standpoint, the rural areas of less developed countries can be

Table 1. Estimated per capita use of energy in rural areas of seven developing countries

	India (1)	China, Hunan (2)	Tanzania (2)	Northern Nigeria (2)	Northern Mexico (2)	Bolivia (2)	Bangladesh (6)
				10^3 Kcal/day			
Human Labor	.67	.64	.64	.61	.75	.71	.67
Animal Work	1.00	.92	--	.13	1.30	1.83	1.00
Fuel Wood	2.86		15.07	10.27	9.70	22.83	.93
Crop Residues	1.16	13.69					1.65
Dung	.67						.57
Total Non-commercial	6.36	15.25	15.71	11.01	11.75	25.37	4.82
Coal, Oil, Gas and Electricity	.53	2.05	--	.02	19.81	--	.27
Chemical Fertilizers	.22	.34	--	.05	5.33	--	.10
Total Commercial	.75	2.39	--	.07	25.14	--	.37
Total All Sources	7.11	17.64	15.71	11.08	36.89	25.37	5.19

thought of as partly closed ecosystems in which
energy derived by people and animals from the
photosynthetic products of plants is used to grow
and prepare food, which in turn provides an essential energy input to grow more food and so on in
an endless cycle. These ecosystems are being dis-
rupted by rapid population growth.

Energy in Seven Countries

Table 1 shows the estimated per capita use of
energy in rural regions of seven developing
countries. To allow an easy comparison with human
food intake the units used are thousands of kilo-
calories per person per day. In India and Africa
the food energy contained in the average diet is
about 2100 kcal; in Latin America, about 2400.
Total energy use is much more than the intake of
food energy, ranging from about 2½ times in
Bangladesh to close to 15 times in northern
Mexico. Except for the latter, most of the
energy is from noncommercial sources; it is provided by the people themselves.

Five different kinds of noncommercial energy
are listed in Table 1: human labor, animal work,
fuel wood, crop residues and animal dung. Energy
provided by human labor is assumed to be about 1/3
of the energy in the food eaten by the entire
population. This assumption is based on a
detailed study of the human energy required for
different agricultural, domestic and other tasks
in rural India (1), in which it was concluded that
between 40 and 45% of the total food energy intake
of adults and older children is utilized in manual
work. The remaining food energy is utilized in
basal metabolism and nonwork activity. Energy
utilized in animal work is estimated to be 40% of
the food energy intake of bullocks and other draft
animals (1). The energy used in human labor and
animal work is relatively small compared to the
energy obtained from fuel wood, crop residues and
dung.

Table 2 shows how energy is used in rural
India and Bangladesh. About 20% of the total
energy is allocated to agriculture. This is
mostly human and animal labor, plus relatively
small quantities of energy from commercial sources,
used for pumping irrigation water and for

Table 2.   Energy uses in rural India and Bangladesh

	India (1)		Bangladesh (6)	
	Total 10^{14} Kcal	Daily per caput 10^3 Kcal	Total 10^{14} Kcal	Daily per caput 10^3 Kcal
Agriculture	2.52	1.57	.333	1.32
Domestic Activities and Food processing	7.31	4.55	.852	3.38
Lighting	0.48	.30	.050	.20
Pottery, Brickmaking & Metal work	0.76	.47	.014	.06
Transportation & other use	0.35	.22	.055	.22
Total	11.42	7.11	1.304	5.18

production of chemical fertilizer. Between two
and three times as much energy is used in domestic
activities as in agriculture, mainly for cooking,
food processing, and procuring fuel. In many
rural areas at least one member of the family must
spend most of his or (usually) her working time
gathering fuel for cooking, and for space and
water heating. Much less energy is used for
lighting and for the traditional energy-intensive
village industries--pottery, brickmaking, metal
work, and blacksmithing--than for agriculture or
domestic activities. Transportation represents a
significant use, but in India it is the least
energy-consuming of all rural uses. In Bangladesh,
energy used for transportation is about equal to
that used for lighting. Most of the energy for
transportation represents animal work, and to a
lesser extent human labor, (people are the draft
animals in much rural transportation) or modern
transport in trucks and tractors.

Table 3 summarizes some of the characteristics
of energy uses in the 7 countries listed in Table 1.
The total per capita use varies widely from about
37000 kcal per day in the relatively modern agricultural economy of northern rural Mexico to about

5000 kcal in Bangladesh. Energy use in the
Chinese province of Hunan is 2½ times that in
rural India. Except for northern Mexico, domestic
uses are much larger than nondomestic uses,
ranging from a factor of slightly more than 2 in
India and Bangladesh to 18 in northern Nigeria and
37 in Tanzania. In these African areas hardly any
animal draft power is used in agriculture, and no
commercial fertilizers.

Nondomestic uses are more than twice as large
as domestic uses in northern rural Mexico because
agriculture has been modernized. Much of the
energy here is utilized in the manufacture of commercial fertilizer, in pumping irrigation water
and in mechanized agricultural equipment (2).
Domestic uses are highest in Bolivia and Tanzania
and relatively high in northern Nigeria and northern Mexico because of the large quantities of wood
used as fuel. In northern Mexico most energy
comes from commercial sources; in the other six
countries noncommercial energy is overwhelmingly
predominant.

One of the energy units tabulated in United
Nations statistics are kilograms or tons of coal
equivalent, taking 7.5 million kcal as the energy
in a ton of "standard" coal. Table 3 shows that
on the average in rural areas of developing countries about 600 kg of coal equivalent are used per
person per year, more than twice what is generally
ascribed to these countries in the United Nations
statistics. The difference lies in our inclusion
of noncommercial energy sources, which are not
tabulated by the UN. On a per capita basis, commercial energy is used principally in urban areas
as may be seen from Table 4 which shows total commercial and noncommercial energy use in urban and
rural areas of India and Bangladesh.

Table 3 indicates that there is a rough relationship between nondomestic energy use and cereal
yields per cultivated hectare. Northern Mexico
and the Chinese province of Hunan, with the highest nondomestic energy use, also have the highest
cereal yields. Cereal yields in India, Tanzania,
northern Nigeria, Bolivia and Bangladesh are very
low compared to those obtainable with modern agriculture. Typical yields in European and Japanese
agriculture and in the Corn Belt of the United

Table 3. Characteristics of Energy use in rural areas of seven developing countries

	India	China, Hunan	Tanzania	Northern Nigeria	Northern Mexico	Bolivia	Bangladesh
					10^3 Kcal/day/caput		
Total use	7.11	17.64	15.71	11.08	36.89	25.37	5.18
Domestic uses	4.85	13.92	15.30	10.51	11.85	23.09	3.58
Non-domestic uses	2.26	3.72	.41	.57	25.04	2.28	1.60
Domestic/non-domestic uses	2.1	3.7	37.3	18.4	.47	10.1	2.2
Non-commerical/commercial	8.5	6.3	No com.	157.3	.47	No com.	13.0
Annual use, Kg coal equivalent	346	858	765	539	1795	1235	252
Cereal yields, Kg/ha.	800	1750	700	900	2750	900	1100

Table 4. Total commercial and non-commercial energy in India and Bangladesh

	India (1)		Bangladesh (6)	
	10^6 Total tons coal equivalent	per caput tons coal equivalent	10^6 Total tons coal equivalent	per caput tons coal equivalent
Total Energy	267	.486	19.5	.260
Urban	115	1.045	1.9	.317
Rural	152	.346	17.6	.253
Commercial	103	.187	2.0	.027
Urban	87	.790	0.8	.134
Rural	16	.036	1.2	.017
Non-commercial	164	.298	17.5	.233
Urban	28	.255	1.1	.183
Rural	136	.309	16.4	.238

States are 5000 to 6000 kg per hectare compared to
700 to 1100 kg per hectare in India, Tanzania,
northern Nigeria, Bolivia and Bangladesh. Some
developing countries, for example Egypt, obtain
yields close to those of the developed countries.
One of the critical differences between the high
yielding agriculture of the advanced countries and
the traditional agriculture of the Indian subcontinent and sub-Saharan Africa is the much larger
use of energy per hectare (but not per ton of food
produced) in the advanced countries.

In contrast, energy use for cooking in the
rural areas of developing countries is higher than
in many United States households, because the
energy is used very inefficiently. Fuel wood, for
example, is burned partly in open fires and partly
in inefficient mud or stone stoves. The fire is
started before the pot of rice (in countries where
rice is the dietary staple) is placed on it, and
the fire keeps on burning after cooking has been
completed. Only a small fraction of the heat of
combustion actually serves to boil the rice; most
of it escapes outside the cooking pot. As a result
the quantity of energy going into the cooking process is about 10% of the total energy in the fuel,
in contrast to about 30% in a modern gas stove (1).
This inefficient use of fuel is likely to have
serious consequences for many developing countries
if their rural populations continue to increase.
The principal source of domestic energy is wood,
the "poor man's oil," and trees and other vegeta-
tion are being destroyed for fuel faster than they
can grow.

Agricultural Need for More Energy

Additional energy is needed in agriculture
for four purposes:

a. to provide a larger and more stable water
    supply;

b. to allow increased application of chemi-
    cal fertilizers, especially nitrogen
    fertilizer;

c. to allow more rapid seedbed preparation;

d. for improved transportation.

Taking India as an example, estimates by the Indian Irrigation Comission (3) indicate that about 10^{14} kcal should be used for pumping water-- 4 times the bullock, diesel and electric power now being used for lifting water. This is equivalent to 620 kcal per day for each person in rural India in 1971 (4).

Chemical fertilizer manufacture is quite energy-intensive, especially nitrogen fertilizer, which requires close to 17500 kcal per kilogram of nitrogen (5). Yet chemical fertilizers are essential if advantage is to be taken of the tropical climate, which allows two or three crops to be grown on the same land each year. Where nitrogen in chemical fertilizer is not available, the land must be left fallow for most of the year, to allow time for the soil bacteria to fix nitrogen from the air. The wasteful use of fallow is one of the principal reasons why yields in the developing countries are so low. Applications of nitrogen fertilizer should be raised to around 100 kg per hectare per crop. With 100 million double cropped hectares in India, 20 million tons of nitrogen would be required, corresponding to 2180 kcal per rural inhabitant per day.

Rapid harvesting and seedbed preparation are necessary if two or more crops are to be grown per year. But the bullocks and other farm animals now used for cultivating the land are often too small, or too weak from malnutrition, to be able to pull the cultivating equipment hard enough and rapidly enough so that the ground can be prepared after harvesting one crop in time to plant another one. Makhijani and Poole (2) estimate that an additional 5×10^{5} kcal per hectare per crop are required in construction and operation of small tractors. In rural India this would amount to 620 kcal per rural inhabitant per day, supposing that 100 million hectares can be double cropped. Cultivation of two crops per year would greatly improve farm employment, probably by   at least 50%, corresponding to an added human energy input of 190 kcal per rural inhabitant per day (1).

Improved transportation is needed to bring off-farm inputs to the farm--fertilizers, pesticides, high-yielding seed varieties, farm tools, farm machinery and knowledge--and to facilitate

exporting part of the crops to cities and towns.
It is obvious that farmers will not be able to
purchase the off-farm inputs necessary for modern
agriculture unless they are able to sell a portion
of their crops to non-farmers. In general, modernization of agriculture demands improved transportation both to lower the cost of getting inputs onto
the farm and the costs of tranportation of farm
products to people in the cities and towns.

The total additional energy requirement would
be more than twice the energy now used in Indian
agriculture. It would then be possible, in principle, to approximate the average U.S. yield of
3.3 tons of food grain per hectare per crop,
instead of the present 0.8 tons. Even with an
assumed yield of two tons per hectare per crop the
increased value of farm production could be about
10 times the cost at 1976 prices of the fossil
fuels used for fertilizer, pumping water, transportation and farm machinery. However there are
problems in the use of fossil fuels, the principal
ones being the difficulties of obtaining foreign
exchange in many developing countries and problems
of transportation and distribution in rural areas.

We need to look for other sources of energy
that can be produced locally. One promising possibility is the use of crop residues. For every
ton of the ordinary indigenous rice grown in India,
Bangladesh, or Africa, close to two tons of straw
are produced, with the same energy content per ton
as the rice. In modern agriculture about half as
much energy is used (not counting solar energy) as
the energy in the food produced. Thus crop residues contain about 4 times as much energy as the
amount needed for modern agriculture. If these
residues could be processed to produce the kinds of
fuels needed, viz., liquid or gaseous fuels, even
at a 40% loss of energy in the process, there would
still be roughly twice as much energy available as
that required for modern agriculture. But this
would be true only if the energy used in domestic
activities could be greatly reduced, i.e., domestic
energy could be conserved.

Conservation and Storage

For energy conservation, perhaps the most
important single development would be not a new

source of energy but a better stove, a better way
of cooking food, a cheap and inexpensive, easily
used device that would enable the efficiency of
fuel use to be raised from 10% or less, to 30 or
40%, as it is in a modern gas stove in the United
States--at least a gas stove without a pilot light.

Problems of energy storage must be solved if
local energy sources are to be fully utilized.
The requirement for storage arises because both
the uses and the energy sources are intermittent.
Energy must be stored to obtain synchronism
between the uses of energy and the sources of
energy. One way to store energy is in chemical
fertilizers and other chemical products. Another
is in hydrogen, methane or alcohol. Another is by
pump-back storage of water into reservoirs.
Another may be the use of solar energy pools of
hot water.

The Hills of Nepal

The problems of energy use in rural areas are
particularly critical in mountainous regions. In
the hills of Nepal the people have traditionally
terraced the lower valley areas and hillsides to
make them flat for better cultivation. As the
population has rapidly grown in recent decades the
people are making desperate efforts to grow more
food, with the result that areas that should not
be cultivated are being used for agriculture.
Terraces are being constructed further and further
up the hillsides on steeper and steeper slopes, in
some places all the way to the top of the hillsides. Rainwaters during the monsoon season run
off on the backsides of these terraces and form a
slippery surface between the terraces and the hill.
And as a result landslides occur in which the terraces are destroyed and the soil is denuded.
Driving west from Kathmandu for 40 or 50 kilometers one sees many landslide scars where the
whole side of the mountain has simply slid down
and destroyed any possibility of agriculture.
Even where landslides do not occur, the terraces
are being rapidly eroded, and the numerous streams
that lace the hill country are choked with sediment during the monsoon season. When these
streams debouch on the Ganges Plain of India, the
sediment load is dropped, and the rivers are
diverted from their courses, causing devastating

floods that are becoming more common and more
severe each year. At the same time pasture lands
in the hills are being over-grazed, and forests
are being rapidly destroyed for fuel wood and for
forage for livestock.

What is happening in Nepal is happening
equally in the mountainous regions of India and
Pakistan, and in Latin America. Because of rapid
population growth, the need to produce more food
is becoming greater each year, and because it has
not been possible to increase the very low yields
per hectare, cultivation is being extended to
unsuitable, easily eroded areas. The resource
base for agriculture is literally being destroyed
and the future looks very grim indeed. But it may
be possible to solve the problem by introducing
new sources of energy. In the Nepalese hills two
sources might be combined: small-scale village
hydropower plants and plantations of fast-growing
trees. These possibilities were explored at a
recent conference in Nepal, sponsored by the
Council on Science and Technology of His Majesty's
Government of Nepal and the Asia Society.

From a technological point of view, farming
should be concentrated on the lower terraces near
the valley bottoms. With irrigation and sufficient fertilizer it should be possible to raise
yields during the monsoon season and to grow a
second--possibly even a third--crop on these lower
terraces during the dry season. If hay could be
cut from the pastures during the monsoon and dried,
it would provide feed for livestock in the dry
season, and the over-grazing of the pastures and
destruction of trees for forage could be curtailed.
If the livestock could be kept in pens and fed on
hay, the nitrogen in their urine (2/3 of the total
excreted) as well as the nitrogen in the dung could
be recovered to fertilize the fields.

So far as is known, Nepal has no deposits of
oil, coal, or natural gas which could serve as a
feed stock for nitrogen fertilizers. It does
possess abundant limestone. The relatively small
amounts of fertilizers now used are imported from
India or from world suppliers through the port of
Calcutta. Very few roads exist in the hill
country, and imported fertilizers must be carried
on human backs to most villages. Even at quite

high production costs, fertilizers manufactured
locally in each village would be economical.

For the average hill village of 250 people,
50 tons of milled rice or corn would provide the
basic staple for an adequate diet. At a yield of
two tons per cropped hectare, this quantity of
cereals could be grown on 12 double-cropped hectares. About 2 tons of nitrogen in chemical
fertilizer would be required to obtain these
yields, in addition to the nitrogen in animal
dung and urine. Irrigation water would need to be
pumped from the rivers for the second crop during
the dry season, plus supplemental irrigation in
the monsoon season. With an average pumping lift
of 15 meters, the energy required for pumping sufficient irrigation water would be around 10,000
kilowatt hours. An equal amount of energy would
be needed to lift domestic water supplies 300
meters. This is estimated to be the average elevation of village houses above the river bed.
Using the old electric arc process, which requires
about 45,000 kwh per ton of nitrogen, 2 tons of
nitrogen in chemical fertilizer could be produced
for an energy expenditure of 90,000 kwh. This
process generates large quantities of waste heat
which could in principle be used for drying hay.

The required amount of energy, about 110,000
kwh, could be provided by a 15 kw hydroelectric
plant operated for 310 days a year. For an installation utilizing high-head (about 100 meters) and
small flow, the estimated cost of turbines and
generators would be $7,500. The cost of the
"civil works," utilizing buried PVC pipe to transport water from a simple "run of the river" intake
to penstocks giving 100 meters of head would be
$22,500, or a total cost of $2,000 per kilowatt
for turbines, generators, and "civil works." The
entire installation, including the equipment for
electric-arc nitrogen fixation and production of
calcium nitrate fertilizer, using the abundant
limestone to combine with the nitrogen oxide provided by the electric arc process, could be
operated by one or two retired Gurkha soldiers.
These retired soldiers have gained considerable
familiarity with simple machinery during their
period of service in the British army. After
retirement, they often utilize this experience to
establish and operate small industries in the more

accessible parts of the hills.

The problem of energy for cooking and heating water could probably best be solved by establishing plantations of fast-growing trees in each village. The existing forests used for fuel wood consist of very slowly maturing trees, which do not produce new growth rapidly enough to meet the village needs--hence the present rapid depletion of the forests. Each hill villager uses about three quarters of a ton of fuel wood per year, or about 185 tons per year per village of 250 people. With fast growing trees, this quantity of fuel could be provided on a sustained basis by a 30 hectare fuel wood plantation. The estimated cost of a forest plantation of this area would be around $20,000, including fencing to protect the young trees from livestock.

The total cost per village of a hydropower and fertilizer installation, plus the forest plantation would be approximately $60,000, or $250 per inhabitant of the hills, a total of 1.5 billion dollars for the present population of 6 million people. This cost appears to be very high in view of Nepal's extremely limited resources, but it could be more than justified by the probable reduction in flood damage in India's eastern Ganges Plain, let alone the conservation of agricultural soils in the hills of Nepal. From Nepal's standpoint, the investment might be considered a social cost, to be borne by the government in the same manner as the cost of roads and schools.

A serious social problem might be expected, however. It is likely that the lower terraces, on which production should be concentrated, belong to the richest groups in the villages, while the higher terraces, which should be abandoned, are the source of livelihood for the poorest village groups. To ensure social equity, it might be necessary to supplement provision of small-scale hydropower installations and forest plantations by strong governmental action, such as rigorously enforced land reforms, which would allow a sharing of the benefits by all the inhabitants of the villages.

More Energy for Rural Industries

With the small and decreasing size of agricultural land-holdings per farm family and the growing numbers of rural people without land, it will probably be impossible to raise rural average incomes to a satisfactory level unless employment can be increased through development of small industries in the countryside. At the same time, the agricultural modernization that can result from increased energy supplies for agriculture will facilitate development of agriculture-related industries in villages and small cities and towns of rural regions, provided that additional energy beyond the needs of agriculture can be made available.

With the coming of electrification to villages in Thikriwala Thana of District Lyallpur in Pakistan, many villagers have been able to install and operate small power looms for production of grey goods, which are shipped to the city for final processing. Elsewhere in Pakistan and India, diesel engines and pumps for irrigation are being manufactured in small machine shops located in the cities and market towns of the countryside. In the Kaira district of the Indian state of Gujarat, the "Amul" dairies provide milk and other dairy products to Ahmadabad and Delhi, and many farmers have been able to increase their incomes by maintaining dairy cattle.

In the small city of Comilla in Bangladesh a foundry and repair shop for irrigation pumps and other agricultural machinery has been established, together with a cold storage plant for potatoes, a meat packing plant and a dairy. Other possibilities for rural industries include: leather and wood working, sugar and flour mills, and food and vegetable preservation. Even electric lights can be used to increase productivity by enabling people in villages and small towns to work at night.

For development of rural industries which can be competitive with some of the more centralized industries of large cities, an essential requirement is relatively low-cost energy to operate lathes, looms and other machinery, and to provide heat for metal-working, dairies, and food-

processing. Here, just as in agriculture, we are
concerned with increasing human productivity by
supplementing (but not supplanting) human labor
with electrical, chemical, or mechanical energy.
In the long run there is no other way to raise
incomes.

References

1. R. Revelle, Science 192, 969 (1976).

2. A. Makhijani and A. Poole, Energy and Agriculture in the
    Third World (Ballinger, Cambridge, Mass. 1975) pp. xv
    and 168.

3. Ministry of Irrigation and Power, Government of India,
    Report of the Irrigation Commission, 1972 (New Delhi,
    1972) Vol. 1, pp. 41-56 and 201-246.

4. Office of the Registrar General, Government of India,
    Census of India, 1971 (New Delhi, 1972-75), in various
    parts.

5. D. Pimentel, Energy Use in World Food Production (Report
    74-1, Department of Entomology and Section of Ecology
    and Systematics, Cornell University, Ithaca, N.Y., 1974)
    tables 6 and 15.

6. R. Tyers, Energy in Rural Bangladesh (Harvard Center
    for Population Studies, 1976) mimeographed report.

2

Solar Energy in the
Less Developed Countries

George O.G. Löf

There are two primary reasons that solar energy has not
been successfully applied in the developing countries of the
world. The first reason, applicable also to the developed
world, is that solar energy is expensive. Although "raw"
solar energy is essentially free, when converted to a useful
form, it is one of the most expensive sources of energy we
have.

The second reason for lack of success in applying solar
energy in the developing countries is a poor understanding of
needs in those areas, particularly among solar energy specialists. Since needs have not been identified and assessed,
assumptions pertaining to solar applications have been faulty.

My remarks are directed mainly at these two problems
which impede application of solar energy in the developing
countries. I shall discuss a number of examples that illus-
trate these points. I would like to divide potential solar
applications into two main categories; first the heat applications, and then, secondly and briefly, the uses for work
or electric power.

Why is solar energy expensive? Let me begin my answer
by providing a few numbers. In a reasonably favorable
climate for space heating in the United States, or in any
other favorable solar climate where space heating is needed
for more than half the year, about one and a half therms
(150,000 Btu) of useful heat can be supplied per heating
season per square foot of solar collector. That is equivalent to about a gallon and a half of fuel oil at normal
efficiency of combustion. For solar water heating, a year
around need, nearly four therms can be usefully delivered per
square foot of well-designed collector per year in a favorable climate. At a near-future cost of buying and installing
a solar water heating system, approaching \$20 per square
foot of solar collection surface, and a ten percent annual
cost of capital, solar heat for this application has a cost
of $\{(0.10 \times 20/400,000) \times 100,000\} = 50$ cents per therm. So,
the cost of solar heat delivered for this continuous use in a

sunny climate should be near 50 cents per therm if the chosen conditions apply. Simpler, home-made hardware might not cost as much, but it usually works badly in the U.S. and it is going to work even less effectively in the developing countries. Although a system at $10 per square foot appears attractive, it is no bargain if it has to be thrown away in three years. And in the developing countries maintenance may be difficult.

Borrowing money at 8 percent interest in a developing country may also be difficult -- 20 percent is a more typical rate. With a $10 per square foot collector, a 20 percent interest loan, and a 10-year amortization period, the solar heat again would be about 50 cents per therm. There does not seem to be much chance of getting the cost below 50 cents per therm for solar heat delivery.

Number 2 fuel oil is about 50 cents per gallon in the U.S., but its price is higher in most other countries. Oil at this price provides heat at about 50 cents per therm. So it looks as though solar heat may now be competitive with fuel oil under particularly favorable solar conditions.

This favorable comparison rests on several assumptions. A continuous use for solar energy was selected. If less than four therms per year are recovered and used, the solar heat cost increases. Solar cooling probably requires heat supply less than a fifth of the time, so instead of recovering four therms per year, perhaps half a therm per square foot is actually used per year. Hence the equivalent cost of the energy delivered is five to ten times higher. A high efficiency system was also assumed, otherwise less than four therms will be delivered. Durability is also important, because the investment will have to be amortized in less than ten years if the system life is short.

Electricity has higher value than heat, so conversion of solar heat to electricity should be evaluated. If we convert one therm (100,000 Btu) of solar heat to electricity with presently available equipment, we will be doing very well if we obtain five percent conversion. So one therm (100,000 Btu) at five percent conversion efficiency will produce one to two kilowatt-hours. If four therms of heat are recoverable per square foot of collector per year, five to six kilowatt-hours of electricity may be obtained per year. The cost of heat for this electric production may be in the 50 cents range, so the heat cost per kilowatt-hour of electricity would be about ten cents. With the additional costs of turbine, generator, and other power plant facilities, solar electricity costs approach 20 cents per kilowatt-hour. There are some places in the world where electricity prices are as high as 20 cents per kilowatt-hour, so solar electricity may be competitive in regions where central station electric power is not available.

Solar energy applications may be subdivided in several ways, and for this discussion, I would like to divide them into the two categories of heat and electricity. Most of the potential uses for solar energy in the developing countries appear to be concerned with heat, so I shall emphasize those applications.

Figure 1 shows a simple type of solar water heater. Residential water heating is a year-round need in the developed countries, and it appears that sanitation, health, and comfort would be improved by water heating in many parts of the world where it is not now being practiced. I say, "appears" because, as a solar specialist rather than an anthropologist, I am not qualified to assess the requirements, limitations, social, economic, and political factors involved in the introduction of new concepts and practices in very different environments. The solar specialists and the experts in such appraisals in the developing countries should jointly attack this important problem.

The photograph is of a unit developed in Japan a number of years ago. A simple plastic bag on a flat roof is filled in the morning with water. The bottom surface of the bag is black and the top surface is clear. The water is heated during the day by absorption of radiation on the black surface, and drained into the tube in the evening for the family bath. It is a practical unit, many thousands were made. The heaters lasted one or two years and then were discarded. Their low cost compensated for their short life, so cost-effectiveness was reasonably good. Now an improved model of greater durability is available.

Figure 2 shows a solar water heater which is commercially made in Australia, obviously much more durable. The solar collector in the glass-covered panel and the storage tank in the insulated jacket provide most of the hot water requirements of a typical family in Australia.

Another Australian model, shown in Figure 3, is even more widely used. The photograph shows a number of panels being tested in an experimental facility. In typical installations, three to six collector panels are connected to an elevated insulated storage tank, in a thermosiphon circulation arrangement requiring no pump. Figure 4 shows a "home-made" solar water heater on an Indian reservation on the California-Arizona border.

Solar water heating is not a difficult technology, as can be seen, but careful attention must be given to numerous requirements. The tubing in the absorber plates must be of corrosion-resistant material, or premature failure will occur. A durable glazing material must be provided for reduction of heat losses, otherwise low efficiency will result. Solar heating is a very "forgiving" technology -- most solar equipment will deliver useful heat, but the attainment of good

Figure 1

Figure 2

Figure 3

Figure 4

Fig. 1. Solar Water Heaters--
  Plastic Bag Type (Japan)
Fig. 2. Solar Water Heater--
  Storage Tank (Australia)
Fig. 3. Solar Water Heaters--
  Collector Testing (Aus-
  tralia)
Fig. 4. Solar Water Heater--
  Site-Built (United States)

performance over long periods with virtually no maintenance
requires careful, capable design.

Another solar heat application is space heating. Although the need for space heating is not great in most of the
developing countries, winter heating is a requirement in many
areas. Particularly in the more developed sections of these
countries, the space heating of public buildings, schools,
and business enterprises which have the capability for under-
writing the cost of the system, appears to be a practical
application of solar energy.

In a commercial U.S. system, shown in Figure 5, air is
heated by passing it through a solar collector. For over-
night heat storage, the hot air is circulated through a bin
of small rocks (pebble-bed) which are heated by the air. When
heat is needed in the rooms, Figure 6, the hot air is delivered by the blower to the living space and then returned
to the collector. Figure 7 shows that, when heat is needed
at night, house air is circulated through the warm rocks.
Finally, an auxiliary heat source is used when there isn't
enough solar heat in storage.

A simpler way of heating a building is used in this
structure in southern France (Figure 8), where a black-
painted, south-facing, thick concrete wall absorbs solar
energy passing through two layers of vertical glass surfaces.
The concrete is heated, and room air circulates through slots
in the bottom of the wall, up the space between the wall and
the glass, and back into the rooms through slots at the top.
This passive system provides partial solar heating by warm
air to the rooms.

Space cooling may be a more important need than heating
in most of the developing countries, but I want to state
again that expert analysis of needs and capabilities is first
required. One method for cooling with solar energy, illus-
trated in Figure 9, is by use of an absorption refrigeration
cycle. The principle is similar to that in the gas refrigerator. For commercial buildings and larger structures in the
developing countries, where cooling is needed, this system
may become practical after further development. It is not
free of electrical requirements, because power is needed for
circulation of heat transfer fluids. This system is in the
development stage so far as solar application is concerned,
and it is going to be some time before we know whether it has
practical application even in the U.S.; until we know that
prospect, we probably will not be able to appraise its potential elsewhere.

A structure combining a greenhouse with a dwelling may
be useful in a developing country. Figure 10 shows a new
building at Colorado State University, comprising a small
dwelling in the rear with a greenhouse in front. There are
about 800 square feet of greenhouse area and 800 square feet

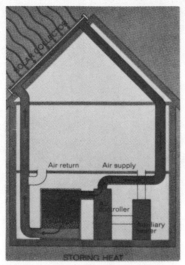

Figure 5

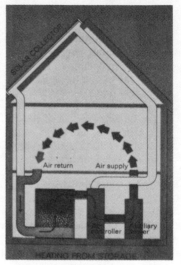

Figure 7

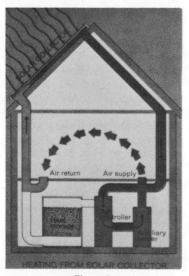

Figure 6

Fig. 5. Space Heating
    with Solar Warm Air--
    Storage
Fig. 6. Space Heating
    with Solar Warm Air--
    Heating from Collec-
    tor
Fig. 7. Space Heating
    with Solar Warm Air--
    Heating from Storage

Figure 8

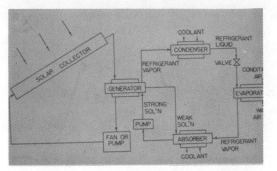

Figure 9

Figure 10

Fig. 8. Solar Heating with Passive Systems
   (France)
Fig. 9. Space Cooling with Solar Energy--Ab-
   sorption System
Fig. 10. Experimental Solar Heated Dwelling
   and Greenhouse (Colorado State University)

Figure 11

Figure 12

Fig. 11. Experimental
Solar Grain Drying
Equipment (Colorado
State University)
Fig. 12. Regeneration of
Batch-Type Refrigera-
tion Unit with Solar
Heat
Fig. 13. Solar Refriger-
ation with Ammonia Ab-
sorption System (USSR)

Figure 13

of living area. The combined use of solar heat in this installation supplies most of the heat requirements of the
dwelling plus part of the heat requirements of the greenhouse.
The greenhouse is double glazed throughout, thereby mini-
mizing heat demand. Food crops are now being produced in this
building, and performance and cost-effectiveness are being
evaluated.

Drying of crops is another use of solar heat. Figure 11
shows an experimental system at Colorado State University
where air is being heated in a solar collector. The hot air
is then used to dry grain in a bin. Crop drying is an ancient
solar application, usually accomplished by spreading the crop
in the field and letting the sun dry it naturally. Losses are
sometimes high by that method and the possibility of increasing food yield by effective drying is extremely important.
Major studies of the potential and practice of this technology are needed.

Refrigeration is another application which is a possibility for the developing countries. Food refrigeration to
reduce spoilage and increase effective productivity appears
to be a need in many regions. Figure 12 shows a small-scale
experiment with a household size refrigerator in which concentrated solar energy is used to generate a refrigerant in
a simple two-chambered device. The refrigerant is generated
for a few hours by distilling it out of a solution in one
vessel into a water-cooled second vessel; after the refrigerant is collected in the second vessel, the device is
lifted from its solar heat source and put inside the refrigerator box. Slow evaporation of the refrigerant then
produces cooling for about a day. This system was used on
some American farms about 50 years ago, with kerosene
supplying the energy for operation. The solar adaptation
is workable but inconvenience and cost are serious impedi-
ments to use.

Another solar refrigeration development is under
investigation in Turkmenia, USSR. Figure 13 shows a flat-
plate solar collector supplying ammonia refrigerant to an
insulated food cooler (refrigerator). Again, high cost is
a deterrent to individual household use. Food refrigeration with solar energy probably has a more practical
application in large central refrigeration plants where
the high capital costs of the equipment can be more readily
borne. Food could be preserved in community-size refrigeration plants by one of these solar-operated methods.

Solar heat can be used to produce fresh water from
salt water. Figure 14 shows a solar water distiller
built in Chile one hundred years ago. It was used to
desalt brackish water at a mining operation in the high
desert. For nearly 20 years, this plant produced distilled water to supply the mules that worked in the mine.

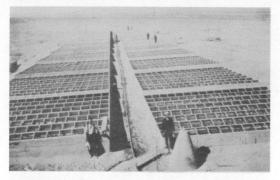

Figure 14

Figure 15

Figure 16

Fig. 14. Solar Distillation of
   Salt Water (Chile, circa 1870)
Fig. 15. Solar Distillation of
   Sea Water (Florida, circa
   1965)
Fig. 16. Solar Still for De-
   salting Water--Under Construc-
   tion (Australian Design, 1972)

A hundred years later this solar still (Figure 15) was built in Daytona Beach, Florida. The design is nearly the same as the Chilean still, but improved materials were used. A shallow basin of salt water is covered by sloping sheets of glass. The salt water slowly evaporates by solar absorption, the vapor condenses on the glass, and the condensed water runs into troughs and out to storage. A portion of the salt water is discharged to waste so that salts will not be deposited in the still. This process has been used for supplying drinking water in a number of parts of the world. Figure 16 shows an Australian design of a slightly different type. Glass covers are supported by two concrete curbs, between which a slab of insulation (to reduce heat loss to the ground) and a waterproof butyl rubber liner are installed. Figure 17 shows the completed solar still. A solar distiller in a sunny climate will produce about 5000 gallons of water per day per acre. The water is expensive, several dollars per thousand gallons, due to the amortization of the relatively high capital cost of the still. But if there is a need for desalted water in quantities up to 25 to 50 thousand gallons per day, a solar still can probably produce it at lower cost than any other distillation method using fuel. Figure 18 shows the dedication of an 80,000 square foot solar still on the island of Patmos in the Aegean Sea a few years ago. There is no source of fresh water on this island except rain water collected on roofs. Although solar distilled water is expensive, it may be the cheapest source.

A Russian solar distiller in Turkmenia (Figure 19), contains a series of ledges over which the salt water trickles and evaporates; the distillate condenses on the glass cover and runs into a separate channel at the bottom. The sloping concrete tray is coated with black asphalt to absorb the radiation.

On the Island of Symi in the Aegean Sea, a solar still recently occupied the only sizable flat area in the town (Figure 20). Plastic film supported by slight internal pressure served as the condensing cover surfaces. Although of lower construction cost than a glass-covered still, this unit deteriorated and failed completely in less than a year. This experience shows the importance of using sound design and durable materials in solar systems, in the developing countries as well as in the industrialized regions of the world.

Solar cooking has long been a popular concept among solar designers. One of the first, Figure 21, was developed by a group in India. This unit was on display at a solar conference 20 years ago. Another type, shown in Figure 22, is an oven with bright metal vanes to reflect solar radiation through a glass cover into an insulated box. In Figure 23, a solar cooker is being demonstrated in a Soviet laboratory

Figure 17

Figure 18

Figure 19

Figure 20

Fig. 17. Solar Still for De-
salting Water--Completed
(Australian Design, 1972)
Fig. 18. Solar Still for De-
salting Sea Water (Potmos,
Greece, 1967)
Fig. 19. Sloping, Ledge-Type
Solar Still (USSR, 1975)
Fig. 20. Plastic Solar Still
(Syme, Greece, 1965)

Figure 21

Fig. 21. Reflect-
ing Solar Cooker
(Indian Design,
1955)

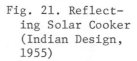

Figure 22

Figure 23

Figure 24

Fig. 22. Solar
Oven (United
States Design)
Fig. 23. Reflect-
ing Solar Cooker
(USSR Design,
1975)
Fig. 24. Solar
Cooker, Concen-
trating Type
(United States,
1960)

Figure 25

Figure 26

Figure 27

Fig. 25. Solar Power Plant (Egypt, 1913)
Fig. 26. Cylindrical Plastic Film Solar Concentra-
tors for Small Electric Power Generator (Israel,
1960)
Fig. 27. Solar Power Generator--Augmented Flat
Plate (Italy, 1955)

near Tashkent. Several small aluminum reflectors focus the
sun on the cooking vessel.
     Figure 24 shows an effective cooker developed by the
University of Wisconsin. The metallized plastic reflector
focuses about a kilowatt onto the bottom of the cooking
vessel. The photograph shows a group of people, mainly
farmers in rural Mexico, watching a cooking demonstration.
Nearly two hundred cookers were distributed and evaluated in
several Mexican communities, with remarkably consistent
results. The cooker was a technical success and a social
failure. The idea failed because people didn't like to cook
in this unfamiliar way. Even though in some areas people did
not have enough food, they preferred to buy kerosene for
cooking what little food they had. Social customs and many
other factors clearly must be reckoned with. I don't think
solar cooking is going to be used anywhere except as a
novelty in the United States.
     Turning now to the other large potential application of
solar energy, we see in Figure 25 the first large solar power
plant built in Egypt in 1913. Long metal troughs focused
the sun on axial tubes in which steam was generated for use
in a pumping engine. This 50 horsepower plant operated a
year or two, but when maintenance became expensive, the
project was abandoned.
     Figure 26 is a photograph of the solar collectors
experimentally used in 1960 for the supply of heated fluid
to a three kilowatt electric turbo-generator designed in
Israel. Cylinders of plastic film, inflated by a bit of
air pressure, are about 30 feet long and five or six feet
in diameter. They focus solar radiation onto a metal tube
in which fluid is heated for delivery to a heat storage
vessel and a small engine.
     About 20 years ago, the solar pump shown in Figure 27
was displayed at an exhibit in Arizona by an Italian company.
Sulfur dioxide was vaporized in the 400 square foot flat-
plate collector and supplied to a reciprocating engine which
drove a one-horsepower water pump. Although hoped to be a
commercial product, high cost forced cancellation of manufacturing plans.   .
     Although numerous solar power generators have delivered
energy, the cost of the electricity produced has been very
high and certainly not competitive with other sources, if
other sources are available. But if power must be supplied
in areas where no other source exists, solar might be a
practical source. Most of the solar electric research effort
in the Soviet Union has been oriented to this objective. If
electricity is needed hundreds of miles from the nearest
power line, much higher costs of site-generated power can be
tolerated. Figure 28 shows one of several types of solar
concentrators focusing the sun onto small receivers in which

Figure 28

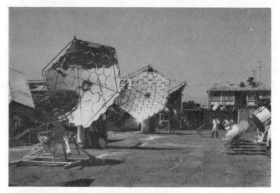

Figure 29

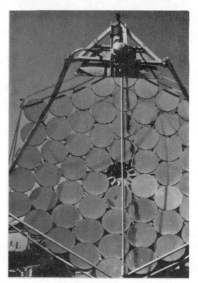

Figure 30

Fig. 28. Solar Power
Generator--Stretched
Plastic Film Concen-
trator (USSR, 1960)

Fig. 29. Solar Power
Generators--Faceted
Glass Mirror Concen-
trators (USSR, 1975)

Fig. 30. Solar Power
Generator--Faceted
Round Glass Mirror
Concentrator (USSR,
1975)

steam or some other fluid is produced. The steam is then supplied to a small engine for electric generation. A thin metallized plastic film is stretched across a dish, on the back side of which slight suction is applied by means of a small pump. The suction pulls the plastic film into a curved contour which focuses the sun on a small boiler. About one horsepower would be developed by this unit.

Figure 29 shows another concentrator, in Tashkent, consisting of an array of glass mirrors that focus the radiation on a boiler which supplies steam to an engine driving a three to five kilowatt generator. Figure 30 shows a variation on this design. Although the USSR is an industrialized country, there are large regions that have the characteristics of undeveloped countries. The prospects for solar power supply in such circumstances need to be thoroughly evaluated.

In summary, it is important to note that, compared to conventional energy technologies in the industrialized countries, solar energy is expensive. However, the higher energy costs in many parts of the developing world make some of the solar technologies currently economically attractive in LDCs. Second, the history of attempts to introduce solar cooking amply demonstrates that efforts to introduce such technologies must take into account not only the economics of a given situation, but also local customs.

3

Photovoltaic Technology

Morton B. Prince

INTRODUCTION

The U.S. National Photovoltaic Program, which is the responsibility of the Division of Solar Energy of the Energy Research and Development Administration (ERDA), will be described with its goals, objectives, strategy, and plans. Since photovoltaics today is relatively expensive compared to other sources of energy, its terrestrial uses are limited today. Some of these applications will be reviewed and shown to be applicable to the developing world. As the cost of photovoltaics is reduced significantly, more and more applications will become cost effective, especially in rural areas in the developing world.

Photovoltaics is the direct conversion of sunlight into electrical energy with no intermediary processes.

Photovoltaic systems offer the potential of clean, highly reliable power. They are capable of operating efficiently in a variety of applications ranging from small, low power devices such as remote instruments, to dispersed systems (residences, shopping centers, schools, industry), to large central power stations for intermediate and peak load operations.

Present sales consist primarily of moderate efficiency, highly reliable silicon-based solar cell arrays, at a median cost of $25,000 per peak kilowatt (kW). Due to the high cost, annual production of solar cell arrays has been limited to several hundred kilowatts.

The cost of photovoltaic systems will be reduced by automation or the use of thin film or novel devices in arrays. However, none of the cost-reduction approaches is sufficiently developed for commercial use, and the market for photovoltaic systems is not sufficiently large to justify additional investment by private industry.

Market information indicates that photovoltaic power can be rapidly expanded both in volume and type of application as the cost of solar cell arrays is reduced. It is expected that photovoltaic arrays can find broad commercial applications if the associated array costs were reduced to the order of $100-$300 per peak kilowatt.

The U.S. Photovoltaic Program is designed to overcome the critical problem of high initial cost resulting in low array production. This will allow for significant growth in the use and application of Solar Photovoltaic Conversion Systems (SPCS).

PROGRAM GOALS AND OBJECTIVES

The overall goal of the photovoltaic program is to develop reliable, low-cost photovoltaic systems and to stimulate the creation of a viable industrial and commercial capability to produce and distribute these systems for widespread use in residential, industrial, and commercial and governmental applications. More specifically, a major goal of the SPCS program is the development and demonstration of photovoltaic systems providing electric energy at costs of 40-60 mills/KWH as compared to present conventional systems costs of 10-30 mills/KWH for intermediate and peak load operations.

In pursuit of these goals, three primary objectives should be accomplished by 1986:

- The reduction of solar array costs to $500 per peak kilowatt with an annual production of 500 megawatts (MW) per year.
- The combined costs of collectors and cells for systems using concentration to be $250 per peak kilowatt.
- The demonstration of thin-film array technology feasibility leading to array costs of $100-$300 per peak kilowatt.

Specific non-technical objectives have also been identified, including studies on:

- Environmental, institutional and legal issues such as the ownership of on-site systems, systems financing, availability of investment capital, sun rights, local building and safety codes, land use restrictions and interfaces with local utility networks.
- Development of performance standards for photovoltaic systems and components that can be used as a basis for warranties, insurance, and consumer protection legislation.

It is anticipated that achievement of the primary objectives will make photovoltaic systems economically competitive (for selective applications) with alternative energy sources for on-site residential and industrial applications, as well as for central power generation.

STRATEGY

As indicated, the cost of photovoltaic arrays must be reduced if the market for these systems is to be expanded. Four concurrent sets of activities have been defined to assist in achieving the programs goals and objectives. These activities relate to the use of existing technology to expand the market, development of large sheet silicon technology, thin-film and new material development, and development of concentrators and high intensity cells.

1. <u>Market Expansion of Existing Technology</u> - Market stimulation through government purchase of a significant fraction of early annual cell production is planned. Solar cell manufacturers will thus have an incentive to use more automated, lower cost production techniques.

Government involvement will provide the industry with a large initial market and the public with a basis for technology comparison. The solar cells purchased will be carefully tested, evaluated, and used in various government and non-government applications. It is expected that ERDA purchases of approximately 600 kW through 1978, coupled with purchases by other Federal agencies, should result in a factor of 4 reduction in the present cost of silicon-based solar cells to approximately $5000 per peak kilowatt by 1979. A total government purchase of approximately 11 MW through 1983 is planned. Costs for silicon solar arrays are expected to drop to $1000 per peak kW by 1984.

2. <u>Develop Large Area Silicon Sheet Technology</u> - Most currently marketed photovoltaic systems use silicon-based solar cells which are hand-processed and individually mounted on a supporting structure. Though the technology and operation of silicon solar arrays are well established, present costs limit their application.

One approach to cost reduction is the development of high capacity, low unit cost production techniques for silicon cells. The acceleration of this activity, involving silicon sheet technology, will provide for: (a) an early reduction in production costs of solar cell grade silicon from $65 per kilogram (KG) to $10 per KG; (b) increased efficiency of the solar cell production fabrication (over 75 percent of the silicon material is now wasted); (c) improvement in the ratio of cell to array area (packing factor); (d) development of suitable encapsulation materials to increase array lifetime; and (e) automated production of silicon solar cell arrays.

Production processes, techniques, equipment and experimental process production plants will be developed to support the commercial adoption of silicon sheet technology. It is expected that this process will reduce the silicon-based solar cell array costs to $500 or less per peak kilo-watt.

3. <u>Conduct Thin Film and Novel Materials Research</u> - Use of thin film deposition techniques utilizing silicon, cadmium sulphide, gallium arsenide and other materials may allow the production of solar arrays costing $100-$300 per peak kilowatt. However, the physics, engineering and manufacturing of high efficiency, reliable, low-cost thin film arrays is poorly understood at present. In particular, present thin film arrays have efficiencies of only 3 to 7 percent.

Studies are underway to develop a better understanding of basic processes, fabrication techniques and costs. The objectives of this research are to develop and demonstrate thin-film, 10 percent efficient solar cell arrays by 1980, and to demonstrate the feasibility of $100-$300 per peak kilowatt arrays by 1986.

4. <u>Develop Concentrators and High Intensity Solar Cells</u> - For a given power output, photovoltaic system costs may be reduced by employing solar concentrators to increase the solar energy received by each cell. This reduces the number of relatively high-priced cells required. The use of concentrators, combined with cells from low-cost silicon arrays costing $500 per peak kW, should lead to combined collector/cell costs of $250 per peak kilowatt by 1986. Systems using such arrays may be competitive with conventional power for residential and central station applications. Analyses of concentrators, cells, cooling requirements, and uses of available thermal energy are now being conducted.

ADDITIONAL STRATEGY ACTIVITIES

The program strategy also includes studies to determine the necessary costs for photovoltaic systems for on-site and central station applications. The effects of institutional, legal, and socio-economic factors on the introduction of photovoltaic systems will be analyzed. Parallel design studies of residential, commercial, and central station applications of photovoltaic power will be carried on to define system, subsystem, and component specifications including cost, reliability, performance, and efficiency. Definition planning activities through the 1980's will support and receive input from test activities and the research and development program. These studies will be instrumental in guiding the direction of the photovoltaic program and will aid in evaluating results from tests, experiments, and early applications of photovoltaic systems.

Marketing studies now in progress will estimate the size and characteristics of the market for early applications of photovoltaic power in both the government and commercial sectors. An initial estimate for near-term (1975-1985) applications indicates that wide-spread application of photovoltaic power could include such items as impressed current corrosion protection of gas well casings and gas and oil pipelines, as well as providing power for railroad crossing signs, navigational buoys, and highway signs. Applications such aś water sampling systems, food and medicine refrigeration, and security surveillance systems are under consideration for implementation on a cost-sharing basis.

New and more detailed market and mission studies are being initiated to: (a) define the domestic and foreign market for photovoltaic systems as a function of system cost, performance requirements and uses; (b) define the technical, financial, institutional, legal and local factors affecting photovoltaic system acceptance; (c) analyze certain potentially attractive applications to define modifications in existing design approaches; (d) develop and maintain a plan that defines the necessary activities, responsibilities, and actions for the successful commercialization of poten-tially attractive applications; (e) evaluate the effects of the introduction of photovoltaic systems on the size and characteristics of the photovoltaic market; and (f) assure effective implementation of commercialization activities.

These marketing studies will develop a description of the application and market potential of photovoltaic systems. Necessary technical developments, required changes in institutional, legal or local conditions, and required experimental pilot and demonstration facilities and activities will be delineated.

PROGRAM PLAN

The Photovoltaic Conversion Program is designed to expand the commercial use of photovoltaic systems as rapidly as possible through research, process development, testing, and application. The cost and risk of photovoltaic systems, both to potential purchasers and the Federal government, will be limited as a result of this program. By encouraging government purchase of a significant fraction of the early annual solar cell production, ERDA will provide industry with the incentive to adopt low cost production techniques. Industry will be able to produce solar cells at decreasing cost per peak kilowatt.

The development of automated processes and experimental production facilities will aid industry in reducing solar array production costs. To take advantage of the understanding of silicon cell technology developed over the past 20 years, emphasis will be on the development of processes that can provide low cost silicon solar arrays. In addition, reduction of solar array costs through the use of thin film deposition techniques and novel materials and devices, and development of concentrating systems will be pursued.

Early residential, commercial, and other applications of photovoltaic systems will be implemented to develop information on operational costs, reliability, and performance, and to acquaint potential customers with the characteristics and feasibility of such systems.

APPLICATIONS SUITABLE FOR RURAL AREAS OF DEVELOPING COUNTRIES

ERDA has been pursuing early low power applications for photovoltaics that could be useful for rural areas in developing countries. This work has been done primarily through the NASA/Lewis Research Center (LeRC). In addition ERDA has been interacting with the World Bank and the Agency for International Development (Department of State). These latter organizations have been involved in searching for low cost, reliable power supplies to help upgrade the quality of life in developing countries. The LeRC has been cooperating with these organizations and with the U.S. Department of Interior, Bureau of Indian Affairs on similar activities for our own Indian reservations. The results of testing on the Indian reservations will be applicable to many other parts of the rural world.

One of the earliest experiments carried out by the LeRC was in India with the Satellite Instructional TV Experiment (S.I.T.E.). Panels of photovoltaic cells were used to charge batteries for powering village television sets for receiving instructional material from a stationery satellite. The experiment was concluded last year when the satellite was moved and the test was considered successful.

Another useful application for rural villages is the solar powered refrigerator. Two installations have been made in the United States as part of the ERDA program. These are small (4 ft^3) camper size refrigerators used to hold medicines such as vaccines and other perishable items. One installation was on a remote island in the Isle Royale National Park in upper Michigan for supplying a construction crew. The second is operating in a rural health dispensary on an Indian reservation at Sil Nakya in the south part of Arizona. Each is powered by a 200 watt photovoltaic panel.

Under consideration for development are shallow well water pumps powered by photovoltaics to supply water for human and animal consumption. Also under consideration is a photovoltaic powered cereal grinder. These latter two applications would relieve the rural villagers of the tedious work of drawing water and grinding meal and allow their time to be spent on more productive activities which in turn could help improve their quality of life.

Several developing countries have indicated that they would like to encourage tourism to remote village areas but that tourists are reluctant to stay at such areas without a modicum of their normal comforts. By powering small appliances with photovoltaics it is expected that tourism could be increased with the villagers benefiting from the resulting commerce.

All of the above applications require daily energy in the 100 watt-hour to 10 kilowatt-hour energy range. Photovoltaic power systems capable of delivering such energy requirements are available. However the cost of such systems leads to problems in most capital scarce developing countries since these photovoltaic systems are associated with up-front costs. Even though the operating costs of such systems are minimal due to lack of fuel needs, the initial investment requirements does pose a serious problem.

With the cost reduction program under way at ERDA, this problem will be reduced significantly during the next ten years.

4

Alternative Energy Technologies in Brazil

José M. Miccolis

Introduction

It is imperative that Brazil consider alternative
energy production and conservation techniques in order to
cope with one of the most demanding crises of its modern
history: the so-called "energy crisis." To mention just
one of the most serious consequences of the current situation, Brazil imports about 650,000 barrels of petroleum per
day, which accounts for more than 78 percent of total consumption, at an annual cost of more than 3 billion dollars.
Oil amounts to 50 percent of the total energy utilized in
Brazil. Over the past few years several steps have been
taken in the direction of reducing Brazilian dependence on
external sources of energy. Alternative energy production
technologies have been examined. Some of them are very
promising medium-term solutions, and are mostly in the research and development stage. Others offer attractive
short-term possibilities and are currently in the initial
stages of implementation.

Energy conservation measures that have been undertaken
in the past three years have not been very successful.
Despite sharp rises in fuel prices, internal consumption
is rising consistently at a rapid rate. More recently,
however, the Brazilian government has enacted much tougher
conservation measures that are expected to change substantially the energy consumption pattern in the country.

This paper is an attempt to report the major alternative energy activities underway in Brazil. Due to the
range of possibilities which could be considered, and the
limited amount of time and space available, relevant technical details will not be included; such details are, however, available upon request.

The Brazilian Energy Picture

Natural Resources

Brazil's waterpower resources are among the greatest in the world, with an estimated potential output equivalent to that of 4.5 million barrels of oil per day. While the installed capacity of generating plants increased from about 7 million kilowatts in 1964 to 22 million kilowatts in 1977, the vast majority of Brazil's estimated 120 million kilowatts is still untapped. The potential sites are distributed all over the country. The Northern region, where the Amazon basin is located, accounts for about 40 percent of that total; the densely populated and impoverished Northeast has 11.3 percent; the South and Southeast, the most prosperous and industrialized regions in the country, have 48 percent, of which most of the economically feasible sites will be totally tapped by the year 1985. The Amazon tributaries located on the north border of the river would alone be able to meet Brazil's requirements over the next several decades. However, transporting this energy to the main energy-consuming centers about 2000 miles away poses several technological problems which are yet to be resolved.

While water power resources are abundant, petroleum and natural gas reserves are relatively small. Total proven petroleum reserves are estimated at 780 million barrels, with additional investigations now taking place on the continental shelf. Usable natural gas reserves are calculated at 15 billion cubic meters (530 billion cubic feet).

Suitable coal reserves, mostly in Southern Brazil, are estimated at 2.2 billion tons, and total reserves at about 4 billion tons. The additional reserves consist mainly of high ash, high sulfur coal which yields a low-grade fuel.

It has been determined that shale deposits extend from Southern Brazil right up to the Amazon basin. Estimates indicate that shale reserves could be the source of 3.1 billion barrels of shale oil.

Uranium reserves are estimated at between 7500 tons and 12,000 tons. Newly discovered radioactive anomalies in Northern Brazil show definite signs of potentially large uranium deposits. Thorium, an alternative material to be used as fuel for gas-cooled high-temperature nuclear reactors, can also be found in large monazite sand deposits, as well as in niobium deposits that are estimated to be from several hundred thousand to about one million tons.

Energy Supply and Demand

Table 1, below, shows Brazil's changing reliance on various energy sources from 1952 to 1972.

Table 1. Energy sources in Brazil (1).

Energy sources	1952	1972
Coal	6.1%	3.6%
Petroleum	28.0%	44.8%
Gas	0%	0.3%
Hydroelectric Power	11.2%	20.8%
Other Fuels	54.7%	30.5%
Firewood	(49.9%)	(27.0%)
Sugar Cane Bagasse	(2.1%)	(2.0%)
Charcoal	(2.7%)	(1.5%)
TOTAL	100.0%	100.0%

Overall, energy consumption has tripled in absolute value in this 20-year period. Petroleum consumption increased from 128.9 million barrels in 1964, to 302.4 million barrels in 1974, of which 78 percent was imported. The petroleum industry is under fairly extensive government control through Petrobras, the government-owned oil company which has almost full responsibility for exploration, production, and refining of petroleum in Brazil. Private enterprise accounts for 12 percent of the country's refinery output. The Brazilian government has recently signed "risk contracts" -- in which the government shares in any profits, but does not incur losses -- with foreign oil companies for drilling on the Brazilian continental shelf.

Electricity consumption in Brazil has grown in the period from 1968 to 1975 at an average annual rate of 11.8 percent. The electricity generating capacity, over the same period, has increased at an average annual rate of 12 percent. In 1975, the overall installed generating capacity was almost 20,000 megawatts, of which 82.7 percent was hydroelectric and the remainder thermoelectric. Also in 1975, total electricity consumption was about 68 million megawatt-hours. Thus, for a population of little more than 100 million people the per capita consumption was about 650 kilowatt-hours, or 14 times smaller than that of the U.S. Overall energy consumption has been growing at a rate of 6.5 percent, well above the rates for the U.S. and Europe. Table 2 shows on a percentage basis the Brazilian energy market in 1970.

Table 2. Brazilian energy market in 1970 (2).

Uses	% of Total	Uses		% of Total
Agriculture	5.79	Transportation		22.03
Fishing	0.19	Highway	18.25	
Mining	0.30	Railway	1.08	
Industrial	34.35	Oceans and		
Steel	7.70	Rivers	1.57	
Metallurgy	1.82	Air	0.98	
Minerals	5.43	Others	0.17	
Mechanical	1.48	Construction		0.67
Chemical	3.02	Commerce		2.32
Textile	1.82	Services		0.65
Paper & Pulp	2.33	Government Services		2.48
Food	8.98	Domestic		31.22
Others	1.75	Urban	12.50	
		Rural	18.71	

In 1975 Brazil agreed with West Germany to purchase a complete nuclear fuel cycle. The terms of the purchase include a joint effort to mine Brazil's uranium and thorium resources, and to design, build, and test eight nuclear power plants totalling 10,200 megawatts. It also includes transferring the technology for the construction of both uranium enrichment and fuel reprocessing plants in Brazil. The reactors will be light water reactors, using enriched uranium as the fuel. The Brazilian Atomic Energy Authority has set a target of 70,000 nuclear megawatts to be installed by the turn of the century.

Alternative Energy Production Technologies

Solar Energy

Brazil occupies a vast region in which solar energy is conveniently available. The country encompasses an area of more than 8.5 million square kilometers, almost entirely located between the Equator and the Tropic of Capricorn. Solar energy is now considered capable of playing an important supporting role on a medium- and long-term basis in the country's energy matrix, since the economic comparisons that always made it unwise to convert solar energy into other forms of energy are no longer valid. Although several scattered efforts to develop solar energy applications in Brazil occurred before 1973, by the end of that year the first comprehensive government attention was devoted to solar energy with the creation of a task force, within the government's planning structure, to examine all possible

alternative energy technologies that could be applicable to
the Brazilian situation. Solar energy was chosen as one of
the potentially successful candidates. A national solar
energy research and development plan was prepared by the
task force, and following approval by the proper authorities
resources were allocated and the plan's implementation
started by the end of 1974.

The underlying philosophy of the R&D plan for solar
energy in Brazil took into account several different
factors: socio-economic and natural resources particular
to the country, which differ from region to region; the
immediately available and easily improvable capability of
local research institutions; and what appeared to be the
state-of-the-art of solar energy conversion techniques at
that time.

The plan's budget for the period 1974-75 was 2.5 million
dollars, in 1974 prices, and focused mainly on solar energy
conversion processes that could be classified as "low-
technology" applications. Some basic research was also
funded. The main projects within the plan are listed
below. A list of participating research institutions is
available upon request. The first Brazilian national
solar energy research and development plan consists of the
following projects:

Collectors. Design, construction of prototypes, testing
and evaluation of flat plate collectors. Determination of
best geometry, materials, configuration, and costs.

Dryers. Design construction, and testing of small-scale
tropical fruit dryers. Identification of fruits more
suitable to the process. Establishment of quality control
standards for the end products. Development of prototypes
of industrial scale agricultural product solar dryers
(e.g., cocoa, coffee, manioc, wood, beans, and grain)
equipped with air preheaters and functioning by natural or
forced convection. Studies of mass and heat transfer
processes involved in solar drying.

Distillation. Development of a small-scale still for
brackish underground water. Testing of different systems
and construction of modular prototypes. Feasibility studies
for the construction of a middle-sized solar still to serve
small communities. Cost-comparison studies of solar distillation versus rain collection and water purification methods.

Refrigeration. Construction of an absorption cycle solar
icemaker, for application in food preserving. Technical
and economic evaluation. Construction of a demonstration
scale solar-cooled food storage facility for semi-perishable
agricultural products such as potatoes, onions, garlic and
other vegetables.

Bioconversion. Experimental tests and feasibility studies
of different processes for high water content bio-mass
fermentation. Anaerobic fermentation of solid organic
wastes. Feasibility studies of the pyrolysis of organic
matter.

Solar architecture. Design, construction and testing of
low-income housing units, exploring locally available
materials and architectural concepts suitable to prevail-
ing climate conditions. Incorporation into the architectural design of solar energy devices like water heaters,
organic waste recyclers, and solar stills.

Thermal engines. Development of a low-power organic fluid
Rankine cycle solar engine for water pumping. Testing of
commercially available systems.

Photovoltaics. Basic research on phenomena of the inter-
actions of photons with matter. Investigation of photocells with polycrystalline structures.

Energy storage. Study of low temperature energy storage
systems. Research on heat transfer processes for water,
air, rocks, plastics, metals, and eutectic salts.

Solarimetry. Rehabilitation of existing solar energy data.
Mapping of monthly total solar radiation for the whole
territory of Brazil, by means of both direct and indirect
data. Establishment of a new solar radiation measurement
network of ground stations.

Ocean Thermal Gradients. Harvesting the solar energy
collected and stored in tropical waters (Ocean Thermal
Energy Conversion: OTEC) has received considerable attention
in the U.S. in the past few years. A heat engine can
operate by means of using warm surface water as a heat
source, and the much colder deep ocean water as a heat sink.
The idea is not technically new and it seems feasible with
current technology. Some regions along the Brazilian coast
present optimum natural conditions for the development of
this process. In the Cabo Frio region of the Brazilian
coast, east of Rio de Janeiro along the Tropic of Capricorn, the deep sea water, cold and nutrient-rich, comes to

the surface. An attempt will be made to generate power
using this water, related to an aquaculture research project which is also using this water for ice making, and as
a basic feed for its marine cultures.

Wind Power. Although windmills have been traditionally
used in some regions of Brazil, regional wind patterns are
not well known. A small-scale research project aimed at
developing a vertical axis (Savonius) wind conversion system
is underway.

Solar Energy Perspectives. If solar energy is going
to play any role in the Brazilian energy picture, then the
Northeast would have to be considered as the most suitable
region for successful solar energy applications. Occupy-
ing a considerable portion of the Brazilian territory, the
Northeast includes all of the country's semi-arid region,
where droughts are common, heavy rains occur within a very
short period of time, and the average daily temperatures
are very high. Furthermore, even measured by Brazilian
standards, the Northeast is an underdeveloped region. The
average annual per capita income is well below the national
level, birth and mortality rates are rather high, the
economy is basically rural and based upon an outdated
ownership and land use model. The national solar energy
research and development plan took into consideration all
these factors. That is why several projects were recommended
and funded: solar stills for areas where an adequate source
of fresh water is not available, and where it is not relevant to make economic comparisons with technologies that
cannot even be applied; crop dryers designed so that a
variety of crops, maturing at different times, can be dried
in sequence by use of the same equipment; solar refrigeration intended primarily for food preservation and for the
storage of seasonal and perishable crops; water pumping
with small solar engines for irrigation purposes; and
others.

The program has thus far failed to accomplish the
development of most of the prototypes intended for an
eventual industrial production and commercialization in
Brazil. This failure cannot be attributed merely to the
fact that only two years have passed since the initial
projects were funded and that, naturally, some projects
have been more successful than others. It was also in part
due to a lack of coordination among several government
agencies which could have taken a much more active role in
the process. For example, the federal housing agency in
charge of financing thousands of low-income units throughout Brazil could have made economically feasible the

large-scale production of solar water heaters to replace the
widely used, inefficient, and electricity-hungry electric
resistance water heaters. Simply by changing current building regulations and by incorporating into construction costs
and financing the added costs for the solar heater, an
insured market would have existed, thus creating an incentive for industrial production of solar heaters. The
government could also have provided incentives for the replacement of conventional fuels with solar energy to provide the low-temperature process heat used in several industries.

Bioconversion is another very promising solar energy
conversion technology. Due to recent developments in
Brazil and to the considerable attention that it has recently received, bioconversion possibilities in Brazil will
be discussed as a separate topic in this paper.

Bioconversion

Green plants are known to be able to capture the sunshine and convert it into stored chemical energy, usually
but not necessarily in the form of carbohydrates. Currently,
with the stored production of ancient photosynthesis --
fossil fuels -- running out, it appears that harnessing the
renewable energy stored in green plants is not only highly
desirable but increasingly feasible. The stored chemical
energy can be recovered by different processes, at the end
of which solid, liquid, and gaseous fuels, as well as
chemical feedstocks and other products, can be obtained.

Brazil is in a very privileged position to make use of
this natural energy collection process, not only because
Brazil occupies a huge area where the incident average solar
energy is abundant, but also due to particular local conditions such as a satisfactory combination of appropriate
soils, water resources and rainfall needed for growing green
plants. Furthermore, the labor-intensive characteristics
of the related agricultural processes, coupled with the
availability of relatively inexpensive and arable land,
could very well match the socio-economic requirements of a
developing nation like Brazil. It should also be noted
that due to the extensive forest resources that are available in Brazil, it is quite probable that a number of other
possibilities might exist in addition to the ones that are
mentioned here. However, the possibilities described below
do represent current knowledge and give a fairly accurate
view of projects under consideration or presently being
carried out.

Fuels and Chemical Feedstocks from Sugar Cane. Since
early in the sixteenth century, sugar cane has been one of
the major Brazilian agricultural products. In 1972 Brazil
became the world's largest producer of cane sugar (6 million
tons per year), with about one-third of domestic production
going for export. High prices in world markets during 1973-
1974 stimulated further increases in production to a level
of 7.2 million tons per year.

--Ethyl Alcohol--Among the many by-products of the sugar
cane industry, ethyl alcohol or ethanol has been traditionally obtained in Brazil by fermentation of surplus molasses
from sugar manufacture and used as an adjunct in gasoline.
The percentages of alcohol in gasoline have varied over the
years (2 to 15 percent alcohol content); ethanol has served
as a regulatory device to maintain a reasonable and profitable level of sugar cane production in the country. Whenever there was a surplus of sugar, the production of alcohol
was increased and greater amounts added to gasoline.

Over the past several years ethyl alcohol production in
Brazil has oscillated between 570 and 700 million liters
per year (150 to 185 million gallons), of which about half
was anhydrous (for mixing with gasoline).

Measures recently taken by the federal government have
insured the sugar cane growers that whenever it is possible
to obtain ethanol or sugar from a sugar cane crop, both
commodities would be worth the same; that is, the price is
set so that the 90 kilograms of sugar or the 30 liters of
ethanol obtainable from 1 ton of sugar cane yield the same
monetary return.

Those measures are clearly designed to stimulate
ethanol production in the country, and are tied to an am-
bitious plan to have 75 percent of the total liquid fuels
consumed in Brazil replaced by ethyl alcohol. According to
one scenario being considered, domestic petroleum production
will increase from the 1975 level of 200,000 barrels per
day to 500,000 bpd in 1980, and to 1 million bpd in 1990,
remaining at that level to the year 2000. In the first
phase (to 1980) ethyl alcohol would be blended with gasoline
at a 1:10 ratio, which does not require any major adjust-
ments to automobile engines. In the following decade,
engines would be gradually adapted to use pure alcohol so
that by 1990, 50 percent of all liquid fuels could be replaced by ethanol. By the year 2000, ethyl alcohol would
account for 75 percent of the country's consumption of
liquid fuels (3).

In order to achieve the goals set forth by the plan, about 400 new distillaries would have to be operational by 1980, 1,150 by 1990, and 3,500 by 2000 (4). This assumes distillaries of an average capacity (12,500 liters/day) and harvesting periods of 160 days. It should be noted, however, that of the approximately 200 sugar mills that are responsible for the current sugar production in Brazil, more than 50 percent are operating at only marginal profits.

Ethyl alcohol has further useful properties. Blended with gasoline, it increases the octane rating of the fuel, thus reducing the need for cyclic hydrocarbons. Also, as an anti-knock additive, ethanol makes the use of lead unnecessary. As a pure fuel, ethanol does have a lower energy content per unit weight than does gasoline; however, the energy content per unit weight is not the determining factor for the power generated by an internal combustion engine. Factors like the heat of combustion, thermal efficiency, etc., are important. When these factors are taken into account for gasoline and for pure ethanol, it is clear that ethanol generates about 18 percent more power. That is one of the reasons, by the way, that several racing engines use ethanol as a fuel. Ethanol consumption, though, is about 50 percent higher than gasoline consumption in a conventional, unadjusted automobile engine. However, for higher compression rates, about 10:1, and with some pre-heating of the air-ethanol mixture in the carburetor, ethanol consumption has been experimentally demonstrated to be about 15 to 20 percent higher than that of gasoline (5). It should also be noted that an ethanol-fueled engine drastically reduces the emission of pollutants such as nitrogen oxides, carbon monoxide, and cyclic hydrocarbons.

Brazil is considering not only sugar cane as the source for ethanol. Cassava, or manioc, a root crop that grows everywhere in the country, has been the focus of considerable government attention, and will be discussed later.

Just recently the Brazilian government approved about US$500 million for implementation in 1977 of a National Alcohol Program that includes both sugar cane and manioc as raw materials for ethanol production.

--Other Fuels--Besides ethanol, a number of other fuels could be obtained from the sugar cane biomass. By means of thermal conversion processes, the fiber could either be used as a boiler feed (combustion), which is currently done in Brazil and which makes the sugar cane industry practically self-sufficient in energy, or converted to synthesis gas by means of processes such as Bailie, Kellog, Koppers-Totzek,

Syngas, Purox, etc. Synthesis gas is a mixture of carbon
monoxide and nitrogen with smaller proportions of water,
carbon dioxide, ethane, and propane. It can be directly
used as a low BTU gas, or processed into a pipeline gas
(methanation), and/or methanol and a motor fuel by processes
such as Fischer-Tropsch, Mobil. Also, by microbiological
conversion techniques, similar to those used for the fermentation of molasses or cane juice into ethanol, substitute
natural gas (SNG) could be obtained by fermenting the
bagasse (6).

   --Chemical Feedstocks--A number of chemical feedstocks
are obtainable from sugar crop biomass. Through fermentation the sugar cane juice, or the surplus molasses, can be
transformed into acetone, isopropanol, butanol, butadiene,
ethylene, acetaldehyde, acetic acid, xanthane, and several
other polymers (7). Some of those products would require
an initial fermentation and additional chemical synthesis
steps, for which the technology is already available.
Furthermore, recent advances in the field of microbial bio-
synthesis that make possible the production of a specific
organic chemical by microbial fermentation could indeed
shorten the additional chemical synthesis steps that are
currently necessary, dramatically changing the economics
for the production of those products.

   --Other Products by Fermentation--Sucrose is an excellent raw material for fermentation. Together with starch
and starch-derived sugars it served well as a feedstock for
the microbial production of several chemicals. During the
post-World War II petroleum-glut period, many of these fermentation processes were discontinued in lieu of lower-cost
petroleum-based chemical syntheses. However, some products,
such as citric acid, penicillin and other antibiotics not
readily derived from petroleum, continued to use fermentation as their commercial source. Since raw materials
account for at least 60 percent of the total cost of the
average fermentation end product, the low cost of petroleum
led to the demise in 1945-1973 of many fermentation processes.

   It must also be mentioned that for the most part the
current reconsideration of fermentation does not yet take
into account the new capabilities of present-day micro-
biology. Rapid, automated, systematic, genetic strain
improvement skills can now replace improvement efforts that
were formerly the province of chance. Achievements in the
antibiotic field stand as evidence of such claims.

While an in-depth study is needed to determine for
local Brazilian conditions the best of the many specific
product opportunities, numerous candidates may be suggested
for consideration: amino acids, such as L-lysine,
L-methionine, L-tryptophan; vitamins like vitamin C
(ascorbic acid), vitamin B12 (cyanocobalamin), vitamin B2
(riboflavin); food chemicals such as acetic acid, citric
acid, nucleotides, and microbial polysaccharides; antibiotics like penicillins G and V, tylosin, gentamicin,
and the cephalosporins (8).

--Ethyl Alcohol from Manioc (Cassava)--Manioc is a
large, somewhat bushy herb which grows everywhere in Brazil.
The roots, which have the appearance of sweet potatoes,
yield a starchy product. Although 2.1 million hectares
were planted in 1973, no commercial-scale operations have
been established. All the manioc is grown in small farming units, manually planted and harvested.

The starch content of manioc, about 25 percent, is far
greater than the 13 percent sucrose content in sugar cane.
The result is that a ton of manioc yields considerably more
ethyl alcohol than does a ton of sugar cane. However, one
hectare of sugar cane crop yields about 50 tons of cane,
and one hectare of manioc yields only about 15 tons.

Manioc crops for energy purposes present problems related to mechanization, and to the fermentation process
itself. Since starch cannot be directly fermented, it
requires enzymatic action, and there is a lack of industrial
experience with its processing. Furthermore, an overall
energy balance would probably reflect the fact that the
manioc industry cannot benefit from burning the residues of
its industrial processing, as the sugar cane industry does
by burning bagasse.

Anyway, manioc crops are very much within the government
plans for ethyl alcohol production. A pioneer manioc dis-
tillary is being built, a fairly large manioc research program is under way, and official estimates assume an increasingly large contribution of manioc to alcohol production,
even surpassing that of sugar cane in less than a decade.

--Socio-economic Considerations of Ethanol Production--
Brazil has abundant land and can continue expanding its cultivated cropland at present rates for most of this century.
Thus, a major agricultural issue consists of finding ways to
make the land resource contribute more toward raising
national and per capita incomes. Brazil is currently dependent on foreign petroleum, for which the country has to

pay about 10 million dollars per day, and it needs to change
both the pattern of the farm labor force, which constitutes
a disproportionately large component of the low-income group,
and to modify somewhat land ownership distribution. Therefore, it is not only very welcome, but necessary, to expand
acreage for energy crops, and thus cash crops.

Estimates indicate that more than 200,000 people are
directly employed by the sugar cane industry in Brazil,
including factory, sugar cane farm, cane and sugar transportation, and other service workers. Most of these people
reside in the areas in which they work. Given the government goals for ethyl alcohol production, and the increasingly larger contribution of manioc, by 1980 about 700,000
new hectares will be planted, with the corresponding settle-
ment of 65,000 farm worker families; by 1990 about 9 million
new hectares will be added to production and 730,000 families
will be settled; and by 2000 there will be 18 million new
hectares and 1.4 million families (9).

Considering that the growth rate of another cash crop,
soybeans, has been an amazing 34.8 percent per year over
the period 1967-1972 (about 5 million hectares), the goals
set forth by the plan do not seem unattainable. Much to the
contrary, they represent a unique opportunity for tackling
the problem of poverty in the agricultural sector, for em-
barking on a land redistribution program, and for implement-
ing a large-scale credit program for the acquisition of
agricultural machinery, fertilizers, and other modern agricultural inputs. Such development offers the possibility
of solving most of the current problems caused by petroleum
imports which are now facing the Brazilian economy.

The economics of ethanol production in Brazil are such
that right now its market price is highly competitive with
that of gasoline. However, there are many different and
attractive technologies and products which are alternates
to obtaining ethanol from sugar cane, and which should be
considered together with ethanol production for the establishment of a more complete and efficient industrial complex.
A comprehensive feasibility study is very much needed. Raw
material considerations, disposition of by-products, marketing of all products, costs of different processes, availability of appropriate technologies and overall energy
balances are but a few of the topics that should be investigated.

Additional Bio-Conversion Alternatives. --Charcoal--
Charcoal produced by carbonization of wood is widely used
in Brazil as a raw material for the production of pig iron

and steel.   Currently more than 2.5 million tons of pig iron
and more than 1 million tons of steel are produced in this
manner in the state of Minas Gerais alone.

Due to the limited availability of Brazilian coal and
its characteristics (it is mainly high-ash, high sulfur
content, low-grade coal), charcoal production will have to
be increased by more than two-fold in the next five years.
However, production methods still being used are quite outdated. By switching to the more modern technique of wood
distillation, considerable amounts of various by-products
could be obtained. For example, from the production of 1
million tons of pig iron using charcoal, it is technically
feasible to recuperate 146,000 tons of fuel gas, 18,000 tons
of acetic acid, 12,000 tons of methanol, and 70,000 tons
of tar, which add up to an additional value of about 200,000
dollars (10).

A fairly comprehensive feasibility study encompassing
different aspects of charcoal production has been conducted
for the state of Minas Gerais. Commercial charcoal production utilizing more appropriate technology will follow.
Furthermore, considering the very extensive forest areas
that are currently being cleared for agricultural production
(more than 2 million hectares in the northern state of Para
alone), wood pyrolysis could be of significant value in the
overall Brazilian energy matrix.

--Hydrocarbon Producing Plants--Hydrocarbon (rubber)
producing plants that naturally grow in the Amazon basin are
being considered as a potential source for the direct photosynthetic production of hydrocarbons. It has been suggested
that proper manipulation of rubber tree (Hevea) production
could control the molecular weight of its principal hydro-
carbon product, polyisoprene, which has a chemical composition similar to that of petroleum, thus obtaining a renewable
"fuel" tree (11). This is still only a research idea. However, other Euphorbia species (of which there are more than
3000 different species in Brazil), like the Euphorbia Tiru-
calli, are also potential candidates for this kind of chemical manipulation and are being investigated.

--Waste Recycling--Organic wastes might prove to be of
considerable significance on the local level for supplying
energy whenever large waste concentrations occur within a
relatively small area. A project that includes the future
construction of a pilot plant for pyrolyzing the municipal
solid wastes of the city of Rio de Janeiro (5 million habi-
tants) is currently in the stage of feasibility studies.

Pyrolysis consists of heating organic material at high temperatures for a prolonged period of time in the absence of
oxygen. Different combinations of gas, oil, and residues
can be obtained, depending on the organic waste composition,
and on the temperature, pressure, and duration of the process.

The anaerobic fermentation of sewage is another way of
disposing of organic wastes. The methane produced by bacteria (typically 60 percent methane and 40 percent carbon
dioxide) can provide the energy needs of the sewage treatment plant itself, or be used as a pipeline gas. The residues, unfermented sludge, can be used as a fertilizer. The
process is simple; presently it is being used in several
locations in the world, and could contribute to the overall
economic feasibility of treating sewage in Brazil. Small-
scale sewage digestors are now being built for future larger
scale developments.

--Water Hyacinth/Fresh Water Algae--Water hyacinth, or
Eichhornia Crassipes, is widespread in tropical and sub-
tropical regions. Submitted to anaerobic digestion it
yields methane and carbon dioxide. Fresh water algae, like
Chlorella, can grow in a sewage oxidation pond, and are
readily subject to bacterial attack. Algae are also a good
protein source, and can be grown very efficiently, with
productivity greater than that of agriculture, although at
somewhat higher costs. Experiments with water hyacinth and
fresh water algae anaerobic digestion are being conducted in
Brazil to determine both their possible use as a fuel and as
a protein source, and the possibility of growing them in
sewage oxidation ponds.

The Hydrogen Economy

Although not exactly an energy production technology,
the "hydrogen economy" was chosen to be included with other
production technologies since its appropriate uses can result in a very interesting, almost unique, possibility for
Brazil. Due to the huge waterpower resources available in
Brazil, and due to the large distances between the major
electric energy consumer centers, hydrogen was initially
regarded as a possible "energy vector" that could conveniently solve the energy transportation and storage problems
associated with those conditions which are almost peculiar
to Brazil.

However, studies conducted in 1974 by the above-
mentioned task force on alternative energy technologies
concluded that other useful hydrogen characteristics should

be regarded on a priority basis for a short-term R&D program, and that they would be more readily applicable to satisfying the national needs.

The National Hydrogen R&D Program was completed in the beginning of 1975. It incorporated two different but inter-related lines of projects: research projects, and technical-economic feasibility studies. The former was intended to foster research both in some frontier areas and in some established areas in which the development of Brazilian know-how was thought to be necessary. The latter was designed to answer questions concerning the applicability of already available technologies and processes to short-term industrial developments.

The Program was approved for its implementation in a two-year period. A list of projects follows. A list of participating research institutions is available upon request. The Brazilian National Hydrogen R&D Program consists of the following projects:

Feasibility Studies:

Primary Electricity Production for Electrolysis:
For already-developed or under-construction hydro-electric power plant sites. Data gathering and estimation of water availability based upon historical data series. Availability of electricity generating equipment. Price of electricity projections for hydrogen production by electrolysis, both for peak and off-peak conditions. Feasibility of using already-developed or under-construction power plants for supplying necessary electricity.
For non-developed potential waterpower sites. Site location. Feasibility of A.C. and D.C. electricity generation at those sites. Economic studies for construction of a power plant specifically designed for providing electricity to a nearby hydrogen facility.

Hydrogen Production. Study of electrolytic hydrogen pro-duction techniques and associated costs.

Hydrogen Transportation:
For short distances. Feasibility studies for building a hydrogen pipeline of about 200 kilometers in a site where hydrogen is currently used as a feedstock for different industries (São Paulo).
For long distances. Development of a computer model for assessing technical and economic variables of a 500 to 1500 kilometer hydrogen pipline.

Hydrogen Storage:
For gaseous hydrogen. Studies of natural formations like
caves and depleted oil and gas wells, for gaseous hydrogen
storage.
For liquid hydrogen. Costs and processes for storage of
large quantities of liquid hydrogen.

Hydrogen Utilization:
As an industrial feedstock. Studies related to the supply-
demand market of hydrogen as an industrial feedstock.
For ammonia production. Processes and cost estimates for
ammonia production from electrolytic hydrogen. Economic
comparisons with alternative processes. Site location for
an ammonia plant using pure, electrolytic hydrogen as a
raw material.
As a fuel. Testing of different kinds of pipelines for
urban distribution of gaseous hydrogen. Feasibility of
supplying a more hydrogen-rich street gas mixture, and of
introducing exogenous hydrogen into the conventional street
gas production processes.

Research Projects:
Production. Evaluation of existing electrolysis installations. Optimization techniques. Research on electrodes
and catalyzers.

Storage. Processes and containers for liquid storage.
Metal hydrates.

Transportation. Material for pipelines. Compressors suitable for hydrogen pipelines. Development of hydrogen-
compatible plastic materials.

Utilization. Catalytic burners. Conventional burners.
Industrial catalyzers. Hydrogen-fueled engines.

Demonstration-experimental facility. Construction of a
laboratory scale facility for testing hydrogen production,
storage, utilization, and transportation, of different
processes, methods, and according to various end uses.

Preliminary Results and Future Trends of the Hydrogen
Program. Petroleum and fertilizer imports are causing an
extremely acute balance-of-payments problem for Brazil. As
a natural consequence, a major portion of the hydrogen
program effort has been dedicated to studying the feasibility
of producing ammonia from pure electrolytic hydrogen. The
results of several studies conducted by FINEP indicate that
ammonia production near a hydroelectric power plant is

competitive with the naphtha reforming process currently
used in Brazil, provided that electricity could be supplied
at a cost of about 12 mills per kilowatt-hour (at 1975
prices), and provided that the plant would produce at least
600 tons per day of ammonia (12). Even for an ammonia
plant located up to 400 kilometers from the power station,
and thus from the hydrogen producing plant, the studies
found that for an installation producing in excess of 1000
tons per day, the ammonia so obtained would still be
economically competitive with that from other processes.
Those conditions (12 mills/kwh electricity, proximity to a
power plant, and ámmonia production of more than 600 tons/
day) are very much feasible today in Brazil.

Plans are now under way for building an industrial-
scale ammonia plant which, if successful, would constitute
a major contribution of the hydrogen program to the country's
energy and economy picture, and would also serve as a
catalyst for the several other research activities being
funded by the program.

Fossil Fuel Alternative Technologies

Coal Gasification. Coal gasification processes are
under consideration in Brazil. Different technologically
established processes (Winkler, Lurgi, Koppers-Totsek,
Otto) were examined as alternatives for ammonia production,
and for the direct reduction of iron ore in steel production. However, due to the high-ash content of Brazilian
coal (55 percent) it is not at this point clear whether any
one of those applications will find its way from the
feasibility-study stage to the pilot and demonstration plant
scale.

Shale Oil. Petrobras, the state-owned Brazilian oil
company, has developed the technology for shale oil production. A pilot plant (1000 barrels per day) has been
operating for the past several years in Southern Brazil.
Plans were recently announced for building the first
commercial-scale shale processing plant. The plant is
expected to yield 51,000 barrels of shale oil, and 1.8
million cubic meters (63.5 million cubic feet) of pipeline
gas per day. For that production, approximately 112
thousand tons of shale will be necessary. About 94,000
tons of residue will result. An advanced research project
is under way for determining other possible applications
for Brazilian shale, as well as for the residues of shale
oil distillation (polymers, fertilizers, medicines, construction materials, etc.).

Energy Conservation Measures

Forced by the increase in petroleum products consumption, despite stepwise price increases during the past three years, the Brazilian government most recently (January 1977) enacted very tough fuel conservation regulations. Those regulations consist basically of:

Gasoline surtax of about 63 cents per gallon. The surtax is to be returned to the consumer after two years, without any value corrections to compensate for inflation (about 50 percent in 1976), and no interest paid. Gasoline prices, as a result of the surtax, will be about US$2.20 per gallon.

Similar measure for fuel oil. The surtax will be US$21 per ton of fuel oil.

Prohibit automobile circulation in downtown areas in major Brazilian cities.

Closing of gasoline stations all over the country on Sundays and holidays.

The establishment of different working schedules for industry, commerce, and government agencies, including staggered hours.

Raising by 50 percent the toll fares on state and federal highways during weekends.

Incentives for the use of alternative energy sources.

Incentives for the use of electricity as opposed to energy from fossil fuels.

Incentives for the expansion of public transportation systems.

Reduction by 10 percent of fuel bills of government agencies.

Limitation of power output of government automobile engines to 89 HP.

Enforcing the national maximum speed limit (50 mph).

Fining owners of badly tuned diesel engines.

Surtaxing gasoline or diesel oil-fired electricity generators.

Restricting imports of airplanes by the government.

Raising diesel oil prices.

Since those measures were taken quite recently, there is no way to evaluate how effective they really are. Furthermore, it is not very clear at this stage what the meaning is of some of them which were phrased more as recommendations than as regulations. However, it is fair to assume that their reach and potential use open up a wide spectrum of possibilities for stimulating the development of alternative energy technologies in Brazil.

Incentives for the use of alternative energy sources include not only the gradual replacement of gasoline and other liquid fuels by ethyl alcohol, but also the "more efficient use" of other natural resources. Notwithstanding the possibilities that have been mentioned, at this point it is not possible to determine definitively which of them will be developed on a priority basis.

Some implications for conservation can be suggested. Public transportation systems (buses) are responsible for 75 percent of the total number of passengers in the ten largest metropolitan areas in Brazil. Increasing this number, say to 85 or 90 percent, could save an estimated 430 to 640 thousand gallons of fuel per year. Also, increasing the person-per-automobile average number (now 1.35 in the largest metropolitan areas) to 2.0 could save an estimated 10 percent of the total annual gasoline consumption in the country. The government hopes to achieve these goals not only by restricting the use of automobiles in downtown areas, but also by a number of complementary measures such as creating special traffic lanes for buses and car pools, charging special toll fares for cars carrying only one motorist, stimulating the production of electrically-powered trolleys and of small, low gasoline consumption automobiles, increasing parking rates at areas near downtown, and a number of other measures. Also, the federal investment in railroads and construction and in electrically powered railroad equipment will be substantially increased and the highway construction program will be kept at a minimal acceptable level.

Conclusions

The possibilities for developing alternative energy
technologies in Brazil are many and varied. Some of them
are peculiar to the country; others are applicable elsewhere. Some are fairly well-developed and need only be
adapted or improved, to take advantage of local conditions.
Others, although very promising, are still a few years away
from being used on a commercial scale.

Nevertheless, for a country like Brazil, as for many
other countries, there is no simple solution for meeting its
energy needs. Different possibilities, though, are not
mutually exclusive. They should contribute to the overall
solution by solving some specific, local problems. It seems
clear that the country's energy policy cannot restrict
itself to short-term planning in this field. Research and
development efforts have to be considered as an integral
part of the policies being formulated -- which, in all fair-
ness, cannot be said to have happened in the past.

The variety of methods, technologies, processes, and
end-products that appear to be feasible in the Brazilian
case, require a very well-coordinated and executed comprehensive approach toward the problem. A systems treatment
is a must. In the first few iterations, a definite answer
is not going to be found; however, a trial and error process
should be conducive to a much better solution than the ran-
dom approach which results from focusing attention on
isolated alternatives.

References

1. J. Goldemberg, Intersciencia 1, 33 (1976).

2. Brasil, Ministério de Minas e Energia, Matriz Energética Brasileira (1970).

3. Brasil, Ministério da Indústria e do Comércio, O Etanol como Combustivel (1975).

4. J. Gomes da Silva, in Problemas de Energia no Brasil, 108 (Instituto de Pesquisas, Estudos e Assessoria do Congresso, Brasília, 1976).

5. U. E. Stumpf, in Açucar e Alcool um Grande Projeto Econômico do Brasil, 155 (Coperflu, Rio de Janeiro, 1976).

6. Conference Proceedings: "Fuels from Sugar Crops," T-39 (Battelle Columbus Laboratories, Ohio, 1976).

7. Ibid., T-15.

8. W. Amon, Jr., personal interview, Cetus Corporation, Berkeley, California, November, 1976.

9. J. Gomes da Silva, op.cit., 114.

10. J. I. Vargas e J. T. Veado, in Problemas de Energia no Brasil, 108, op.cit.

11. M. Calvin, in Hydrocarbons via Photosynthesis, 19, (University of California, Berkeley, 1976).

12. Brasil, Financiadora de Estudos e Projetos, Estudo de uma alternativa para a Produção de Amonia, a partir da Eltrolise da agua, 28 (outubro 1975).

Bibliography

Energy for Rural Development, Renewable Resources and
Alternative Technologies for Developing Countries.
National Academy of Sciences (Washington, D.C.: 1976).

Goldemberg, J., et al. "Energia no Brasil." To be
published by the Academia de Ciências de São Paulo
(São Paulo, Brasil: 1977).

Miccolis, J.M.F. "Programa de Pesquisas e Desenvolvimento
em Energia Solar no Brasil." FINEP (Rio de Janeiro,
Brazil: 1974).

Miccolis, J.M.F. et al. "Programa de Estudos e Pesquisas
sobre a Economia de Hidrogênio no Brasil." FINEP (Rio de
Janeiro, Brazil: 1975).

Proceedings of the International Symposium on Energy Bioconversion, July 5-9, 1976, Campinas (São Paulo, Brazil:
1976).

5

Wind Energy Conversion in India

Sharat K. Tewari

It appears that practically no serious attempt was made to utilize wind energy in India until the 1950s. While wind power has been utilized in propelling and guiding ships and boats, for several reasons no other utilization of wind energy could develop. One reason probably was the ready availability of animate energy derived from the muscle power of draft animals. Rural India has been utilizing bullock work in transportation, in grinding of food grains, extraction of oil from seeds, in preparing lime mortar used in building construction, for drawing water from wells, etc. With its large rural population, India has been significantly drawing upon manual labour also in several domestic and agricultural tasks. Only during the last two to three decades have electricity and oil been able to make an entry into the rural energy scene. However, conventional forms of energy, both animate and inanimate, suffer from some drawbacks. Energy obtained as human and bullock work is expensive and reliance on this form of energy decreases the opportunities for a more productive alternative activity. Bullock work cannot meet the additional energy needs simply because the number of bullocks have not been increasing. Electricity drawn from the grids is available in only one-third of the half a million villages and it will be quite some time before all the villages obtain electricity under the conventional rural electrification schemes. Utilization of oil for energy generation causes an additional drain on foreign exchange resources apart from having the problems of maintenance and repairs in rural areas. From this very brief description of the Indian energy scene, it could be inferred that there is a

need for deriving energy from alternative sources
for use in rural India. I will attempt to establish here that energy derived from winds is highly
appropriate for use in some applications and de-
serves serious consideration.

In this paper the approach adopted for designing wind energy utilization in India during the
last 25 years will be briefly mentioned. From
this, we shall proceed on to a systematic analysis
for obtaining a rightful place for wind energy in
the energy scene of rural India.

In 1952 a wind power sub-committee was con-
stituted under the Council of Scientific and Industrial Research, New Delhi. This committee recommended conducting wind surveys at several locations, adapting a suitable windmill originally
developed abroad, and simultaneously taking steps
to design a windmill indigenously. The anemo-
graphic records of wind velocity were being obtained at the several installations of the India
Meterological Department. Some of these records
were studied and processed from the wind-energy
point of view. This analysis was conducted at the
National Aeronautical Laboratory and helped in
characterizing locations in terms of annual and
monthly average wind speeds, velocity-duration
curves, frequencies of unacceptably low wind spells,
etc. About 160 water-pumping windmills of the
Southern Cross type were imported in the late
fifties and installed at several locations in the
country. During the 1959-64 period, the windmill
WP-2, indigenously developed at the NAL, was produced in batches and about 80 of these were erected for field trials at several places in the
country. This windmill has 12 blades mounted on
a 5-metre diameter rotor wheel. The cut-in speed
is 8 kph (kilometres per hour) and the furling
speed is about 40 kph. A few electricity generating windmills such as 'Algaier,' 'Dunlite,' and
'Elektro' were also tested for performance in
Indian winds. By 1966 wind power activity was
closed down at NAL.

What were the achievements of this programme,
which lasted just over a decade and operated at
full steam for about 3 years? First of all, it
was established through this programme that windmills are acceptable in the tradition-bound society of rural India. Therefore, if only the wind

energy could match with other alternatives in terms of the economics, its utilization would not present any social problem. Another achievement to the credit of this programme was to map out wind energy distribution for some parts of the country. It was shown that the annual average wind speeds at most places in India range from 9 to 17 kph. However, no serious effort could be made under this programme to identify windy locations apart from what had been indicated from the normal meteorological data.

The optimism of cheap electricity from the grids and a lack of proper appreciation for renewable sources of energy, along with some other factors had led to the closure of the NAL wind-power programme by 1966. The oil price hike after 1973 has been responsible for the restarting of the wind energy studies and a fresh look is being taken at this alternative source of energy. Since then the following studies have been initiated.

1. After the publication of reports from the National Research Council of Canada, a few groups in India, appreciating the advantages of the Darrieus rotor, began constructing its prototypes. At NAL attempts were made to energize a commercially available centrifugal water pump with the help of a 4.5-metre Darrieus rotor. However, even with the addition of two large Savonius rotors co-axially mounted with the Darrieus rotor, it was not possible to obtain the starting torque required by the pump. At the Bharat Heavy Electricals Ltd., Hyderabad and at the Indian Institute of Technology, Madras, projects have been initiated for developing a Darrieus rotor for generating electricity at around one- to five-kW capacity levels. Another programme at NAL is directed towards studying a parallel-blade variation of the Darrieus rotor, thus deviating from the usual catenary shape selected earlier.

2. Another line of development has followed the route of the Savonius rotor. The Application of Science and Technology in Rural Areas (ASTRA) Cell at the Indian Institute of Science, Bangalore has developed a modified design of the Savonius rotor for field trials in a village near Bangalore. A 4 x 3-metre prototype has been fabricated from wood, iron wires, and cloth and it is proposed to couple this with an improvised dia-

phragm water pump.

3.   The third line of experiment has gone in the direction of the Cretan Sail Windmill. Such windmills utilize relatively cheaper materials for rotor construction and provide opportunities for utilizing low wind speeds, and at the same time remain cost competetive. A sail windmill having a rotor diameter of 10 metres was erected at Madurai in 1974 to pump water with the help of a reciprocating pump. Recently designs utilizing efficient sail wings have been finalised for a windmill having a 10-metre diameter and it is proposed to match it with a rotary pump in order to minimize energy losses in transmission mechanisms.

In addition to these, a few other design and development programmes are being carried out, but the types mentioned are quite typical. It should be appreciated that while the design and development of hardware is essential, it is equally necessary to study all related aspects of wind energy in a systematic manner so that an appropriate policy could be formulated at the national level for promoting wind energy utilization. Answers to the following questions are needed:

1.   Which are the applications where utilization of wind energy could be recommended on the basis of its being more appropriate than other alternatives.

2.   Are wind speeds and associated durations as given by a velocity-duration curve for various locations in India adequate for the applications; and

3.   What are the economic implications of wind energy.

The most common method of using wind energy is by conversion into shaft work. Electricity may be derived from shaft work simply by coupling a suitable generator to the windmill shaft. This procedure does not involve any serious losses in energy availability, and overall efficiencies as high as 40% have been obtained for converting wind energy into shaft work. Therefore, such of those applications that depend on shaft work can be readily served through wind-energy conversion. Applications such as water pumping, grinding of

food grains, and other agro-industrial activities
are typical of those for which wind energy can be
utilized.

Wind-energy conversion into electricity
through shaft work could be examined on the basis
of the mode of utilization of electricity in Indian
villages. In those villages where electricity has
been made available, it is a common feature that
over 80% of its consumption is in energizing irrigation pumpsets. The rest of it is consumed in
domestic and street lighting. The use of electricity in cooking, space, and water heating is
practically non-existent.

From this analysis it would appear that wind-
energy conversion could be considered primarily for
providing mechanical work, and if electricity is
generated through this conversion, it is ultima-
tely going to be used mainly for generating mechanical work also. We would now examine the appro-
priateness of other alternatives vis-à-vis wind
energy for generating mechanical work.

Prof. Roger Revelle has calculated that about
9% of the total energy used in rural India is obtained from the muscle work of human beings, and
another 14% is contributed from bullock work.
Even though only 1/10th of the total bullock time
is utilized in raising water, nevertheless their
contribution amounted to as much as 40% in terms
of water lifted for irrigation in 1971. As mentioned earlier, the bullock population is not growing and the incremental energy available from this
source is therefore not likely to be significant,
except for the fact that there is room for more
efficient utilization of the existing bullock
force.

It may be stressed here that energy needs are
going to increase, especially for irrigation facilities required to support medium and high energy-
intensive methods in future, in the place of the
current practice of subsistence agriculture.

The cost of energy derived from manual labour
in tasks like lifting water from wells and canals
is estimated to be about 20 times higher than the
commercial price for electricity. Perhaps human
beings are not best suited for such of those tasks

that could be carried out by utilizing inanimate energy. It is a known fact that a prerequisite for improving the quality of life of human beings is to avoid excessive energy dissipation that takes place in the manual labour deployed, for instance, in water lifting. Therefore, a reduced dependence on this source of energy should be the focal point of an energy utilization study like ours.

India is currently meeting two thirds of its consumption of oil from imports. After the OPEC price hike, curbs were introduced on non-essential uses in order to control the demand. However, the demand is bound to increase in the near future from the fertilizer industry and transportation sector. It is estimated that import requirements would be somewhat reduced with the availability of oil in the near future from offshore wells. Even then, it would be desirable to substitute alternatives such as electricity for oil in applications such as irrigation water pumping. In fact a trend indicating a preferential use of electricity in place of oil for this application was shown to exist even before the oil price hike. The electricity is preferred in villages mainly because it calls for less initial capital from a consumer. Use of diesel-powered pumpsets requires the availability of technical skill for maintenance and repairs, which is not easily available in remote areas. Also it is estimated that the unit cost of electricity obtained by smaller diesel generators is four to five times higher than the price of electricity purchased from the grids. This also explains the preference for centrally generated electricity in comparison with the alternative of using diesel pumpsets or generators.

Of the half-million villages in India, about one third have been covered under the rural electrification schemes. Transmission and distribution networks have to be set up for providing electricity to the remaining villages and this will take time. The villages that have been electrified so far are those that happened either to be located near the larger load centres of cities and towns or were large enough themselves to warrant their own generating facilities. This is clearly indicated from the statistics of rural electrification, which show that about 92% of the villages with population exceeding 10,000 were electrified in 1971 whereas only 12% of the villages with

population under 500 had this facility. Smaller
villages constitute over 60% of the total number
of villages. It is likely that more time would be
required to take electricity to far-flung remote
smaller villages under the conventional practice.

Apart from the time factor, supplying electricity to distant villages results in diseconomies
to the system. Energy losses in transmission are
significant and load factors are rather low - just
about 10%. The rural electrification programmes
have the Government's support on account of social
priorities but probably there are other ways of im-
plementing this programme, apart from the current
practice of distributing electricity generated at
at large power stations. Suggestions have been
made for supplying electricity to a group of villages from aerogenerators installed at the neigh-
boring windy sites. We may like to examine the
economics of such a possibility.

The data on rural electrification in India
show that a 25-kW installed capacity is adequate
for a village with a population under 1000. Under
the current practice a distribution line has to be
run to each village and this distance has been
found to be about 8 kilometers on the average. For
remote villages yet to be electrified this distance
would surely be longer. The cost for laying down
these lines over a given distance and the cost of
transformers and switchgear can be calculated. One
could add to this the bought price of electricity
at the last point on the main network to arrive at
the actual cost of the electricity supplied in a
village. On the other hand one could assume a
reasonable capital cost for a well designed and
mass-produced aerogenerator and arrive at its
annual cost by making assumptions concerning the
cost of its spares and maintenance. It has been
shown on the basis of a comparison of the cost
factors involved with aerogenerators on one hand
and the existing practice of rural electrification
on the other that the former could be economically
competetive in many villages yet to be electrified. However, the optimised cost-effective
aerogenerator is yet to be demonstrated in actual
practice.

Having examined the conventional sources of
energy we may now proceed to study the availability of shaft work or electricity from non-

conventional alternatives, including renewable
ones. Some of the alternatives are: (1) Solar-
energy utilization directly for water pumping and
for generating electricity or shaft work; (2)
liquid-piston pumps operating on bio-gas combustion, or internal-combustion engines operating with
bio-gas; (3) water wheels converting the energy
of river flow into shaft work. These are the promising examples. Out of these the water wheels can
be operated only at those very few villages that
have the advantage of a rapid flowing river or a
stream and we shall not consider this possibility
in our analysis here.

Solar pumps have been designed to pump water
from wells with water levels as deep as 30 metres.
Such pumps utilize flat-plate collectors, an eva-
porator, a condenser, a few valves, and a couple
of water chambers lowered into a well. The capital
cost of such pumps is rather high today as compared
to the cost of water-pumping windmills. The
energy-conversion efficiency of solar pumps is
several times lower than the efficiencies of some
of the well-designed windmills.

Solar-energy conversion resulting in shaft
work or electricity through a turbine and generator has also been suggested for use in rural areas.
The costs and efficiencies of these schemes are
comparatively less favourable than windmills and
aerogenerators. In addition the complexity is
much higher in such conversions of solar energy
while wind-energy conversion remains relatively
simpler.

Cow dung and other animal wastes are currently dried and burnt for deriving heat mainly for
domestic cooking in villages. Conversion of such
waste material into bio-gas through anaerobic fermentation and using the gas so collected has been
shown to be a more efficient technique from the
point of view of energy availability. It has also
been suggested that bio-gas could be burnt in an
internal-combustion engine to obtain shaft work.
Alternatively it could be burnt in a liquid-piston
pump for direct pumping of water. Two issues
confront us here. The first concerns the limited
availability of bio-gas and the other its priorities in utilization. It is estimated that with a
75% efficiency in dung collection, the bio-gas
that can be generated in Indian villages can meet

three fourths of the domestic energy requirements.
Since bio-gas replaces dung cakes that are being
used currently in cooking and water heating, the
bio-gas must first satisfy these requirements.
Therefore, unless additional availability of bio-
gas is assured from sources other than cow dung,
and this is yet to be considered on a serious
basis, it would not be possible to recommend bio-
gas conversion into mechanical work. One must
also consider the thermodynamic losses in energy
availability involved with the energy conversion
from bio-gas into shaft work or electricity.

Therefore, it appears that wind-energy conversion into shaft work or electricity for use in
rural India is the main contender provided the
energy availability from winds can be matched with
demand for energy in the applications. We may now
consider these aspects.

The annual average hourly mean wind speed is
generally used as the parameter for depicting the
wind energy potential for a particular location.
An analysis of the available wind speed data has
indicated that at most places in India this figure
falls in the range of 9-17 kph. While designing a
windmill or aerogenerator one picks up a rated wind
speed at which full rated power is generated. The
rated wind speed is normally higher than the annual
average speed though the number of hours of operation at full output are reduced. For instance, if
one selects a rated windspeed as the one to max-
imize energy availability during a year with a
typical aerogenerator, then the rated speed would
be found to fall in the range of 20-25 kph corresponding with the range of 9-17 kph of annual average speed. The number of hours during any year
when wind speed would equal or exceed this rated
wind speed at a given place would probably fall in
the range of 1000-2000 hours. The question then
arises whether this many hours of operation are
acceptable and also whether wind energy is equi-
tably distributed among the 12 months, or even
better, if it is concentrated in the months from
November to March, as these are the months maximum
irrigation is required. Unfortunately, it is just
the other way about with winds in India. The
three months of May, June, and July account for
about one half of the annual energy availability.
Wind speeds during November to March are relatively
weaker. Therefore, under such circumstances, the

rated wind speeds might turn out to be just about
the same as the annual average wind speed. Under
these circumstances, is the utilization of wind
energy economical or even feasible?

There is no difficulty in utilizing low wind
speeds for wind-energy conversion, except for the
fact that low wind speeds require a proportiona-
tely larger diameter for the rotor in order to
produce a given amount of power. Now the important thing is to ascertain the size of windmill
required and then examine whether this size
happens to be too big to be handled in large
numbers in the villages. It was mentioned earlier
that about 40% of the water lifted in 1971 from
wells was based on bullock or human work. The
statistics indicate that on the average an open
well irrigates an area of over 1 hectare. Using
the data for water requirements per season, we
find that about 0.75 hectare-metre of water is
normally pumped during a four-month season. Assuming the number of hours of operation of a windmill
per season as 500, we find a likely pumping rate of
70-100 litres per minute coupled with a typical
head of 10 metres. This pumping could be obtained
from windmills having a rotor diameter not exceeding 12 metres. This is not at all a difficult
situation.

The important concern then is the economics
of wind-energy utilization. It should be noted
that the worth of utilizing an easily available
source of energy such as winds in a rural community is much higher than indicated in terms of
commercial factors. Availability of energy at the
right time in desired quantities could catalyze
developments that were hitherto just not possible.
Indirectly in commercial terms, the high value
and price of agricultural production more than
justifies relatively insignificant cost of water
pumping. It is expected that the total worth of
wind energy would be high despite some diseco-
omies in its application, as this would be adequately compensated by overriding social benefits.

In conclusion it may be stated that wind-
energy conversion has attractive possibilities in
India and for some applications like water pumping it is perhaps the most appropriate alternative
among the several choices available or likely to
be available in the future. On account of low

cash surplus in villages it might be necessary for
the Government to support wind-energy utilization
in the same manner as the programmes of rural electrification, and the economics of these two alternatives would be comparable. In addition, the
technology of wind energy could be disseminated in
a short period of time owing to its simplicity,
which is not likely to be surpassed by another alternative.

Small Hydraulic Prime Movers for Rural Areas of Developing Countries: A Look at the Past

6

Joseph J. Ermenc

Historical Perspective

The two hydraulic prime movers, which have been important instruments of change in rural areas of developing nations in the past, are the waterwheel and the small water turbine which superseded it during the +19C.

The basic difference between the two is that there is a contrived flow of water with respect to the energy conversion elements (blades/vanes/buckets) of the water turbine and not of the waterwheel.

The waterwheel was the first prime mover used extensively (other than persons and animals). It dominated the power scene for about 2000 years. It was at first integrated with traditional hand-craft methods which led to changing patterns of making and doing things and with revolutionary increases of goods and services. But the power limitations of the waterwheel (less than 20 horsepower) essentially limited the size of these operations. Its use was therefore characterized by a diffusion of mills throughout rural areas. In Europe and the United States this was the prelude to their Industrial Revolutions; Mumford has called this the Eotechnic Phase of a developing country based on wood as a material of machine construction, water as a source of power, and the native craftsman as the dominant technological figure.(1)

During the Roman Empire all species of waterwheels appear in rural areas. They were used primarily for grain and saw mills. A three horsepower (2.2 kilowatts) waterwheel powered grain mill near Cassino, Italy was capable of supplying the flour needs of about 400 people. A conglomerate of 16 waterwheels at Barbegal in southern France supplied power to produce up to 28 tons of flour per day for the

GALLO-ROMAN FLOUR MILL AT BARBEGAL, NEAR ARLES, PRODUCING   28 TONS OF FLOUR PER DAY.' A.D. 308-16.

TWO SERIES OF EIGHT WHEELS; EACH 6·9 FT. (220CM) DIA. AND 28 IN. (70 CM) WIDTH.

TOTAL HORSEPOWER c 170 ; HEAD - 65 FT (20M)
(ISIS , 38 , 1947-48)

FIG. 1

Roman Legions.(2) Though these were examples of the revolutionary possibilities of the waterwheel, vested interests
and social-political restraints seem to have prevented its
wider and more intensive use. (Fig. 1)

The collapse of the Roman Empire and its slave-based
economy swept away the restraints against the use of the
waterwheel in the West.

By the +11C the waterwheel was well established in rural
Europe, driving saw and grist mills and pumping water. Even
in England which was then, in comparison with Europe, considered as a backward country, there were,according to the
Domesday Book of 1085, 5624 water-powered mills operating in
3000 communities in southern and eastern England.

By the +14C Europe was experiencing an escalating use of
the waterwheel in many handcrafts. Two principal stimuli set
this off:

1. The exemplary use of the waterwheel in monasteries.
2. The labor shortages brought on by the Black Plague.

By the +16C, the use of the waterwheel had been extended to such traditional handcrafts as:

1. Mining(drainage, ore transport and crushing).
2. Metallurgy (blast furnace blowers, rolling and strip
   mills).
3. Metal working (forging, turning, grinding, wire drawing); agricultural tools.
4. Woodworking.
5. Leather processing(tanning, harness).
6. Paper making
7. Oil manufacture
8. Cosmetics (powder, perfume).
9. Polishing (lenses, ivory, minerals).

The number of waterwheels in Europe by this time was
reckoned in the tens of thousands. Their site selection, design and construction was attended to by a superior
group of craftsmen called millwrights.(3)

In the American colonies the use of waterwheels begins
within a few years of the establishment of settlements. In
1647, only 20 years after the Pilgrims had landed at Ply-
mouth, waterwheels were used in an iron mill at Saugus,
Massachusetts; here bog iron ore (limonite) was processed
into wrought iron bars (merchant iron) at a rate of eight
tons per week.

But small mills were far more prevalent than the Saugus iron mill. By the end of +18C there were about 10,000 water-wheels in New England driving a variety of mills on tribu-taries of main-line rivers and tributaries of those tribu-taries. It was not uncommon to have a dozen mills on a brook use its entire flow in succession.

In China, the first reference to the waterwheel occurs in +31. It was used for the job of operating an air bellows in metallurgical processing (cast iron and wrought iron) and fabrication (casting and forging). By +230, iron tools became three times as abundant as in pre-waterwheel times.(4)

By the +13C, in the Chinese province of Szechwan, "tens of thousands of waterwheels for hulling and grinding rice, and for spinning and weaving machinery, were established along the canals (in the plain of Chhengtu) and operated throughout the four seasons."

During 1780, a Korean scholar passing through an area 40 miles east of Peking wrote, "I saw waterpower used for all kinds of things; blowing air for furnaces and forges, winding silk off cocoons, milling cereals,. There was nothing for which the rushing force of water to turn wheels was not employed."

So by the beginning of the +19C, areas of Europe, the United States, and China were well prepared technologically to receive the next beneficence of hydraulic power, the water turbine.

(Since World War Two up to a hundred watermills in suc-cession have been seen on small rivers in rural areas of the provinces of Shansi, Kansu, and Yunnan. Some water-wheels, made of wood, have been connected to small electric generators (for lighting) via pulleys, belts, or ropes.)

The water turbine was a French triumph. It was preced-ed by the development of sound turbine theory by French scientists during the +18C. This guided the French engineer, Benoit Fourneyron, between 1825 and 1833, to produce several small water turbines which demonstrated superiority over the waterwheel in almost all respects.(5)

They could operate adequately at higher heads or lower heads than the waterwheel - and even submerged. They could replace the waterwheel at a site and develop twice the power at ten times the speed. They occupied only a small fraction of the volume of the waterwheel. They could also be placed as high as twenty feet above the tailwater (using a draft tube) without appreciable loss of power.

By 1838, the news of Fourneyron's turbine had already reached the United States. A few were built in the Boston area, strictly following Fourneyron's design. But in the hinterlands it was rapidly taken over by blacksmiths and foundrymen who found it easy to make, in great demand and an extremely profitable business. Changes came very quickly and by the middle of the century the Fourneyron turbine had been so radically altered by rural craftsmen that American turbines began to take names of their many improvers. Changes continued throughout the century; during this period there were more than 60 varieties of small, cheap, cast iron turbines on the market as replacements for waterwheels.(6)

Efficiency and cost were often not the main criteria in turbine selection by mill-owners. Many rural New England small mill operators rated turbines on their capability of passing bodies of small animals.

The last quarter of the +19C was the heyday of the small turbine. When a waterwheel needed to be replaced or the power increased at a millsite, a turbine was selected. An 1885 census reported over 900 turbine powered mills operating on the 110 mile long Merrimac River and its tributaries. (The Merrimac River flows from central New Hampshire south, then east through Massachusetts.) The average power of these turbines was about 30 h.p. (22 kilowatts).

The mills were highly specialized and were duplicated at least four times in the Merrimac watershed indicating their limited areas of service.

They turned out such household products as cutlery and edge tools, brooms and brushes, looking-glasses, furniture, paper, buttons, woodenware, stone and earthen-ware, pencil lead, vinegar, combs, ivory and bone-work, toys and games, baskets, needles and pins, watches and clocks, and even washing machines.

For the farm they turned out fertilizers, gunpowder, axles, agricultural implements, barrels, ax handles, wheels, carriages. There were woolen, cotton, flax and linen mills; hosiery, lace, worsted, glove and mitten, mattress, cordage, twine, shoddy and bagging mills.

There were tannery, boot and shoe, and leather-board mills.

There were also mills turning out surgical appliances,

MILLS ON THE THREE MILE LONG NEWFOUND RIVER
IN NEW HAMPSHIRE, 1885

KIND	NUMBER	HEAD	HORSEPOWER
WOOLEN	1	16	30
PAPER	3	40	297
CARPENTERING	2	–	30
FLOUR & GRIST	3	30	130
BLACKSMITHING	1	12	15
WOODTURNING	1	16	30
CARRIAGES & WAGONS	1	12	50
GLOVES	1	18	76
TANNERY	2	38	150
MACHINERY	1	8	2
STRAWBOARD	1	12	–
WOOD PULP	1	22	200
SAW	1	12	50
TOTAL	19		1060

(FROM "REPORTS ON THE WATER POWER OF THE UNITED STATES",
DEPARTMENT OF INTERIOR, CENSUS OFFICE, 1885.)

FIG. 2

musical and scientific instruments.(7) (Fig.2)

After 1900, in the United States, the advent of large
central thermal and hydro-power stations, rural distribution
of electricity, the internal combustion engine, and better
rural transportation all contributed to the decline of the
small turbine powered mill.

Today there is only one nationally known manufacturer
of small turbines in the United States; and the last manufacturer of waterwheels closed shop in 1967.

So in the United States and Western Europe, both Eotechnic prime movers, the waterwheel and water turbine, have
gone through complete cycles of existence from the rise of
invention, development, and acceptance to a gradual slide
into obsolescence just short of oblivion. (Fig.3)

In China, it appears that century of foreign interfer-
ence has delayed the introduction of the small turbine; but
this is now in progress with particular emphasis on small
scale hydro-power stations.

A BBC broadcast, during 1970, informed that thousands
of units of less than 100 kw were being installed in rural
areas. This parallels the installation of small, simple
hydro-electric stations in the United States at the beginning of this century. (10,11,12,13,14)(Fig.4)

Since World War Two, small hydro-electric package units
of less than 20 kilowatts have appeared in West Germany,
Hungary, Canada, Russia, and the United States.(9) But the
cost of these units indicate that Western manufacturers have
priced themselves out the rural market not only in developing countries but in our own as well. But beyond this they
represent refinements unnecessary in rural areas of developing countries and unwise in that their complexity and maintenance is beyond the understanding and the resources of
the rural craftsmen. (Fig. 5,6)

Waterwheels

By the +4C in the Roman West, and perhaps earlier in
China, the waterwheel had evolved into two distinct species
which converted different forms of hydraulic energy into
mechanical energy (force-velocity combinations).

1. The undershot wheel receives energy from the impact
of a flowing stream of water on flat (later curved) radial
vanes/paddles.(Fig. 7)

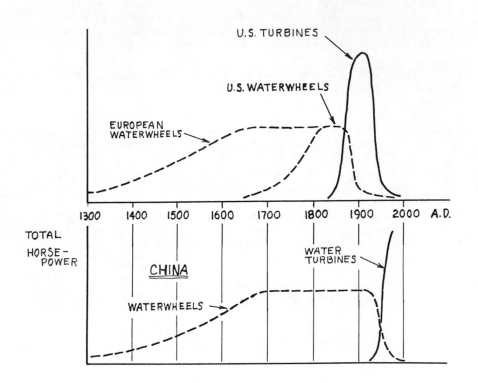

SMALL (LESS THAN 100 HORSEPOWER) HYDRAULIC
PRIME MOVER CYCLES.

FIG. 3

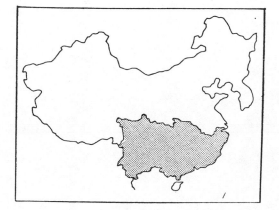

SMALL HYDRO-ELECTRIC STATIONS
(AVERAGING 40 KW)
IN
SOUTH CHINA

(V. SMIL, BULL. ATOMIC SCIENTISTS, FEB. 1977)

FIG. 4

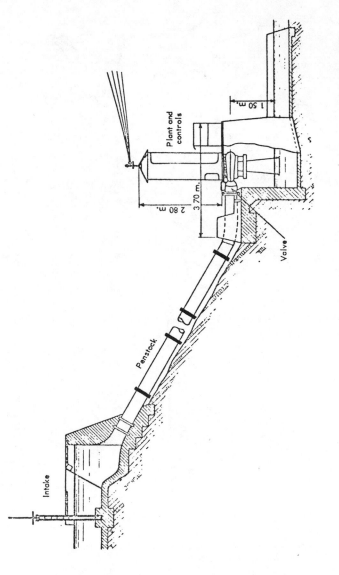

Intake

Penstock

2.80 m.

3.70 m.

Plant and
controls

Valve

1.50 m.

Typical layout of micro hydro-plant. [From: *Small-Scale Power Generation*, United Nations, New York, 1967.
UN Publication Sales No. 67.II.B.7.]

FIG. 5

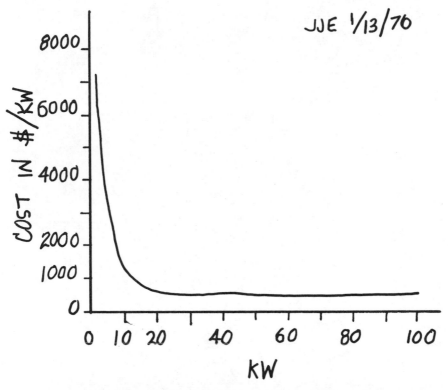

JJE 1/13/70

COST PER KW OF SMALL SCALE
HYDRO-ELECTRIC PACKAGE UNITS
(NOT INCLUDING INSTALLATION
OR DAM COSTS)

FIG. 6

UNDERSHOT WATERWHEEL
OPERATING
AIR BELLOWS FOR TWO IRON HEARTHS
FROM
AUGUSTINO RAMELLI, "LE DIVERSE ET ARTIFICIOSE MACHINE", PARIS, I

FIG. 7

2. The <u>overshot wheel</u> has 'buckets' on its periphery. These are filled at the top of the wheel's rotation and empty as they approach the bottom, (the breast wheel receives water, in buckets, at about radial height). The <u>overshot</u> wheel always rotates in a vertical plane. (Fig. 8)

The <u>undershot wheel</u> may rotate in either a horizontal plane or a vertical plane.

The vertically rotating wheel was the dominant form used in the West though the horizontally rotating wheel was to be found in the hilly regions of the Balkans, France, Italy, Scandinavia, Ireland, the Shetlands, and the Faroes. (Fig. 9)

In China, the horizontal wheel was dominant.

Until the +19C, both types of waterwheel were generally made of wood with cast and wrought iron used sparingly where extra strength or wear resistance was required.

The Overshot Wheel

The overshot waterwheel had an efficiency around 80 percent which was several times higher than that of the undershot waterwheel. Indeed it was often higher than the efficiency of the early small turbines. Further its efficiency remained high despite variations in load imposed upon it; this superior characteristic was not obtained with the undershot wheel or with the early turbines.

For the mill operator the overshot wheel was most economical of water and this explained its use well into the +20C and particularly on small streams. But on the debit side, the overshot wheel was limited to speeds of less than 20 rpm for wheel diameters of 15 feet (4.6 m) and for horse-powers of less than 20 (15 kw). These limits were imposed by the use of wood as the material of construction before the +19C.

Because grain milling required higher speeds than achieved with the conventional wheel, power transmission units had to be inserted between the water wheel and the millstones to increase the rotational speed. The units consisted of gears or pulleys and belts or ropes.

When the available heads were greater than the usual wheel diameters, the overshot wheel was used in series. This was to be seen in surprising fashion at the Gallo-Roman

OVERSHOT WATERWHEEL
OPERATING
A GRIST MILL AND A PISTON PUMP
(RAMELLI 1588)

FIG. 8

HORIZONTAL WATERWHEEL
OPERATING
A GRIST MILL

(RAMELLI 1588)

FIG. 9

flour mills at Barbegal in southern France; they were built
between 308 and 316 AD and represented the largest hydraulic
power plant the world was to see for fifteen hundred years:
the total power developed there was about 170 horsepower
(127 kilowatts).

There were two series of eight overshot wheels, each of
which was geared up to drive two sets of millstones. Each
series of wheels received water from the aqueduct supplying
the city of Arles. They used the water in succession along
a slope of 30 degrees and through a vertical height of about
61 feet (18.6 m). Each wheel had a diameter of 7.2 feet
(220 cm) and a width of 2.3 feet (70 cm). (Fig. 1)

All together they produced 28 tons of flour per day,
mainly for the Roman Legions in southern France. A similar
mass production flour mill was built at Prety in Burgundy
for the Legions of Northern Gaul.

During the nineteenth century the overshot waterwheel,
in responding to demands for increasing power, made
increasing use of iron forgings for axles and hubs and cast
iron for rims.

In 1854 the largest diameter Western overshot wheel was
constructed on the Isle of Man, in the Irish Sea, to pump
water from a lead mine. It was 72 ft(22 m) in diameter,
6 ft (1.8 m) in width. It developed about 125 horsepower
(86 kw) at 2 rpm. It could pump 250 gallons per minute
from a depth of 1200 feet.

In the United States, in 1851, the largest overshot
waterwheel was installed at the Burden Iron Works in Troy,
New York, for the manufacture of railroad spikes. It was
60 ft (18.3 m) in diameter and 22 ft(6.7 m) in width; it
delivered about 200 horsepower at a speed of 2½ rpm.

The Undershot Vertical Waterwheel

The efficiency of the undershot vertical wheel with
flat vanes set in a stream ranged from 10 to 20 percent;
with curved blades this rose to 20-30 percent. If water
was conveyed to either a vertical or horizontal wheel via
a close fitting channel or if the wheel was shrouded to
minimize the effect of turbulency, these efficiency ranges
were doubled. But these efficiencies are maximums which
are attained only when the speed of the wheel is roughly

half that of the approaching stream of water: on either side
of this wheel-speed, the efficiency decreases; this would
happen with variations of load or water supply.

Except for curved blades, the Romans had developed the
undershot wheel with shrouds into a standardized piece of
equipment which often was of better design and construction
than most rural wheels of the +18C. An impression of one in
lava was found near Cassino, Italy. It had a diameter of
6.1 ft (1.85 m), a width of 10 inches (0.25 m) and flat
paddles. It was estimated that this wheel developed about
three horsepower at about 10 rpm. Since millstones required
a higher velocity for some of its products, a set of wooden
peg tooth gears were used which, in Roman waterwheel practice, stepped up the speed by a factor of five. (Fig. 10)

The output of this rural Roman flour mill was estimated
to be 300 lbs (136 kg) per hour. Compared with 20 lbs (9 kg)
per hour which could be done by two men on a quern this was
indeed revolutionary.

A novel use of the undershot water wheel was developed
during a siege of Rome during the +6C. This was the boat/
floating mill. It consisted of an undershot wheel suspended
between two rigidly connected boats. They were widely used
on swift flowing sections of navigable streams in many
European countries and China. It has been estimated that
on the River Po, in Italy at the beginning of the +19C, there
were about 600 boat mills.(8)

The use of boat mills in China begins about the same
time as in the West; on them trip hammers were often used
for such tasks as:

1. Hulling and grinding rice.
2. Pulping fibrous materials for paper.
3. Pulverizing materials for drugs and perfumes.

In the United States the undershot vertical wheel was
used where terrains were unfavorable to the building of
dams to impound water and create heads. In the West, the
Roman noria, the undershot wheel with buckets attached
to raise water, was used occasionally. At Ellensburg on
the Columbia River, two crudely constructed wooden undershot
waterwheels, one of 42 feet in diameter, and the other
30 feet were used to irrigate 40 acres of land for alfalfa
and fruit.

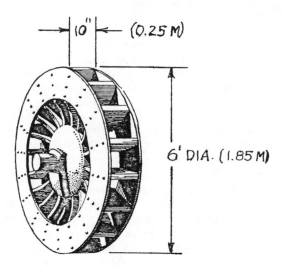

10" ← (0.25 M)

6' DIA. (1.85 M)

ROMAN UNDERSHOT WATERWHEEL (VENAFRO)

3 HP @ 46 RPM → 330 LBS (150 KG) FLOUR PER HOUR
DONKEY MILL → 15 LBS (7KG) " " "

FIG. 10

And some Alaskan Indians constructed wooden undershot wheels of the noria type but with nets instead of buckets. The nets scooped fish out of the water and dumped them into a chute.

Undershot vertical wheels were also used to develop tidal power along the Atlantic coasts in Europe, England, and the United States. They were generally used as adjuncts to inland water mills or windmills.

The Undershot Horizontal Waterwheel

This wheel rotates in a horizontal plane (its shaft is vertical). Water is conveyed to it by an open or closed channel from water at some elevation usually under 10 ft (3 m).

By the +17C, it had evolved into a high speed elementary turbine in southern France, the Balkans, and China. With curved blades it reversed the flow of water to secure a reactive effect which produced speeds four and five times that of vertical wheels. It could therefore be directly connected to millstones and saws without the intermediary gears or pulleys and belts. They also made use of large diameter shafts for their 'flywheel effect' in smoothing out sudden velocity variations caused by vagaries in water flow and load.

Indeed it was the alleged remarkable performance of the horizontal water wheels at the Basacle flour mills, near Toulouse, France, which, during the +18C attracted the attention of such early French hydro-dynamicists as Euler, Bernovilli, d'Alembert. Their studies of this wheel found focus in the invention of the first practical water turbine by Benoit Fourneyron from 1825 to 1833.

During the +19C, horizontal waterwheels using flat blades were used in northeastern United States for grist and saw mills.

In China, as late as 1958, wooden horizontal wheels, with blades of extreme curvature exhibiting high speed characteristics were being built for connection to small electric generators (under 5 kilowatts) via pulleys, belts or ropes.

From 1910 to 1960, a horizontal wheel was in operation in central New Hampshire grinding grain for animal and poultry feed. It is 7 ft (2.1 m) in diameter and received

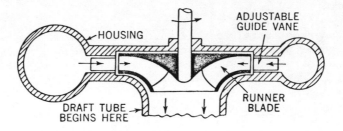

FRANCIS (RADIAL-INWARD FLOW) TURBINE

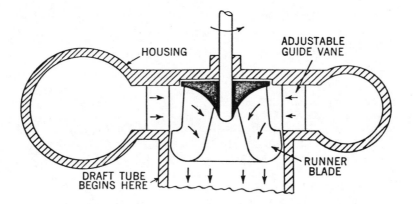

AMERICAN/FRANCIS (MIXED FLOW) TURBINE

FIG. 11

water under a head of 6 ft (1.8 m) through a 2 ft (0.6 m)
square closed channel bound with iron straps. It probably
developed about 10 h.p. (7.5 kilowatts) at 30 rpm. Its
shaft is of steel and 5 inches (12.7 cm) in diameter.

The Water Turbine

The water turbine differs from the waterwheel in that
there is a flow of water relative to the blades/vanes; under
design conditions the water enters the moving blades smooth-
ly and leaves with minimum energy.

There are three well established classes of turbines
which are generally known by the names of their inventors,
developers, or promoters. They are in historical order:

1. Francis (reaction, pressure change across blades,
   full admission, inward mixed-flow). (Fig.11)
2. Pelton (impulse, no pressure change across blades,
   partial admission, tangential flow).(Fig. 12.)
3. Nagler (fixed propellor, or reaction, pressure
   change across blades, full admission, axial flow).
   (Fig. 13.)
4. Kaplan (variable pitch propellor, reaction, full
   admission axial flow.
The Francis, Nagler and Kaplan turbines are propelled
mainly by reaction forces and appear to be lineal descen-
dants of the Alexandrian (Hero/Ctesibius) steam turbine
(-1C or -2C), the first jet engine.

The Pelton turbine/wheel appears to be a descendant of
the horizontal waterwheel but it had an independent con-
ception and development in California following the Gold
Rush of 1849.

The inward flow Francis turbine was a radical trans-
formation of Fourneyron's outward flow turbine to keep it
a high rpm machine while responding to demands for more
power. This was done by keeping the rotor diameter increase
minimal while increasing the rotor (blade) depth. This
resulted in a compact rotor of considerable complexity but
not beyond the fabrication capability of the village black-
smith or small town pattern-maker and foundryman.

It was this small Francis turbine which was the principal successor to the waterwheel in northeastern United
States. Due to its full admission, steady flow features it
was able to approximately double the power of the overshot
waterwheel at a given site where the flow of water was adequate. However on small brooks the waterwheel was preferred

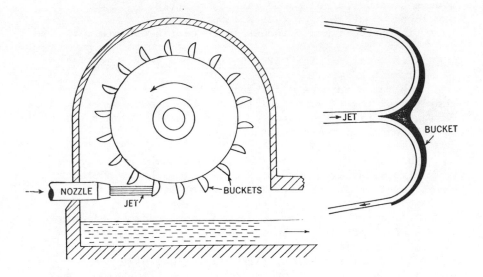

PELTON TURBINE FIG. 12

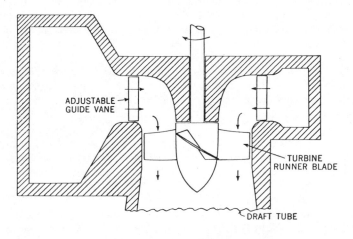

PROPELLOR TURBINE

FIG. 13

because it was more efficient at part loads than the turbine.

The Nagler fixed propellor turbine resembles a ship propellor. This suggests it to be an invention via the inversion method. It is a simpler structure than the Francis turbine and is particularly compatible with the usual waterwheel heads. It came on the scene after World War One with the rise of large central hydro-electric stations and was built for this market as a competitor of the Francis turbine. Its high speed often permitted direct coupling with an electrical generator.

The Kaplan turbine uses a variable pitch propellor. It maintains a higher efficiency under load fluctuations than the other types. But it is mechanically more complex and is generally used only in large hydro-power, efficiency oriented stations.

The Pelton impulse turbine is a partial admission prime mover in which high pressure water is received in a nozzle, converted into a high velocity jet of water and directed onto hemi-spherical blades. It is generally used with heads greater than 100 ft (30 m). Their requirement of long, high pressure pipes/penstocks would preclude their use in many developing countries.

Hydraulic Power Sites

The development of hydraulic power is limited to sites where the evaluation of the following factors must be favorable:

1. Topography (slopes, water storage, evaporation).
2. Geology (run-off, dam sites).
3. Stream flow (rainfall, water shed area).

In developing countries of the past this was done by experienced millwrights; today it is a formalized procedure described in engineering textbooks and handbooks.

The drop in elevation may be of natural origin or artificially created by a dam which also serves to store water. For small mills, economy generally required that the connection (penstock or pentrough) between the dam and turbine or waterwheel be kept a minimum. But with small hydro-electric stations of 1000 kw or less, in New England, it was not uncommon to see penstocks of five and six ft (1.5-1.8 m) in diameter and several miles in lengths.

Log dams of the 'eave' or 'rafter prop' type were generally used in New England. They were cheap and easy to maintain and replace. Their stability was obtained by the weight of water above the 'eave' rather than by the mass of the dam itself. The cost of monolithic concrete or stone dams was generally prohibitive for small New England mill owners.

Summary

The waterwheel and small hydraulic turbine were of basic importance in the development of rural areas of the United States and Europe. Indeed their use may be seen, from an historical perspective, as the springboard from which hydraulically endowed areas were transformed from handcraft economies into diffused machine-based economies with consequential revolutionary increases in the production of goods and services.

The major role in this development was played by the simple waterwheel. The advent of the small hydraulic turbine provided more power at a given site than was feasible with the waterwheel.

The introduction of the small water turbine appears to be taking place in China at the present in much the same way as it did in the United States a century ago. Though large central thermal and hydro-power technology are available to the Chinese, it appears that there is considerable emphasis, at the present, on small hand-controlled machines.

It seems that the history of small scale hydro-power development provides sound suggestions of how to aid hydraulically endowed rural areas of developing countries in achieving an improved standard of life not only for their areas but also for less advantaged areas of their country.

References

1. Mumford, L. 1934, "Technics and Civilization". New York: Harcourt and Brace.
2. Singer, C. 1958, "A History of Technology", Vol.8, Oxford: University Press.
3. Fairbairn, W. 1864, "Treatise on Mills and Millwork". London: Longmans, Green and Co.
4. Needham, J. 1971, "Science and Civilization in China". Vol. 4 Cambridge: University Press.
5. Rouse, H., Ince S. 1957, "History of Hydraulics". State University of Iowa.
6. Ermenc, J.J. 1976, "Dartmouth Readings in Technology: The Historical Development of Water Power". Thayer School of Engineering, Dartmouth College.
7. U.S.Dept. of Interior, Census Office, 1885, "Reports on the Water Power of the United States", Government Printing Office.
8. Bachelli, R. 1950, "The Mill on the Po". New York: Pantheon.
9. Mosonji, E. 1960, "Water Power Development", Vol. 2, Budapest: Hungarian Academy of Sciences.
10. Editorial Publishing Group, East China College of Water Conservancy, Nanking, 1973, "Rural small scale hydroelectric stations". People's Republic of China: Shanchai People's Press (in Chinese)
11. "How to Run Small Power Stations Efficiently". 1971 People's Republic of China: Shanghai People's Press (in Chinese).
12. Canton Bureau of Water Conservancy and Electric Power 1973. "Rural Small-Scale Hydro-electric Stations." People's Republic of China: Canton People's Press (in Chinese).
13. Editorial Publishing Group on Rural Small-Scale Hydro-Power Stations, Bureau of Water Conservancy and Electric Power, Revolutionary Committee of Human Province 1974. "Rural Hydro-Electric Stations", 2 volumes. People's Republic of China: Hunan's People's Press. (in Chinese).
14. New China News Agency, August 1970. "BBC Summary of World Broadcasts", Part 3: The Far East Weekly Economic Report. London: British Broadcasting Company.

7

Wood Waste as an Energy Source in Ghana

John W. Powell

THE TROPICAL HIGH FOREST OF GHANA

Kumasi is the capital of the ancient kingdom of Ashanti which now comprises the Ashanti Region of Ghana. Almost the whole of Ashanti is covered by tropical forests and more than half of the sawmills in Ghana are located in or around Kumasi. It is therefore an ideal location for the study of the tropical high forest and the industries which it supports.

Two important institutions located at Kumasi are engaged on research connected with the cultivation and uses of timber. The Forest Products Research Institute of the Council for Scientific & Industrial Research is the principal institution engaged upon research into the industrial utilisation of the produce of the forests. It is situated on the Campus of the University of Science & Technology which is the only technological university in Ghana and includes a course in Timber Technology among its curricula. The University has established a Technology Consultancy Centre to stimulate the development of small industries through the introduction of intermediate technologies and several of its projects involve the use of wood as a fuel or as a raw material. The present paper draws mainly upon the experience of the Forest Products Research Institute and the Technology Consultancy Centre.

The tropical forests of Ghana cover perhaps one third of the land area or about 30,000 square miles. Much of the remainder of the Country supports more limited tree cover of savanna species. It is variously estimated that between 150 and 300 species of trees grow in Ghana. Of these, only 18 are listed as Prime Species with timber that is acceptable on the international market. Only 8 species account for 70% of Ghana's timber exports. These 8 are Mahogany,

African Mahogany, Wawa, Sapele, Utile, Makore, Kokrodua
and Anthotheca. Although much effort is expended in
attempting to export the so-called secondary species, the
situation is changing only very slowly. It is true therefore to say that the vast majority of the trees growing at
the present time are not used as timber. According to
Siwek[1], about 80% of the Ghanaian species are suitable for
use as fuel wood.

There is no doubt that the land area of the tropical
forest is reducing and has been reducing for several
centuries. The historical cause has been the slash and
burn agricultural practice but in recent years, the timber
companies have taken out trees faster than the reforestation
programme can replace them. The savanna lands drift south-
wards pursued by the Sahara across the whole of the
Sahelian region, and this effect can be seen in Northern
Ghana. There is also no doubt that the ecological balance
is being upset in other ways especially by the selective
re-planting of commercial species in the forest area and
fast growing species for firewood in the savanna area.
However, this consideration is beyond the scope of the
present paper.

THE TIMBER INDUSTRY

According to Siwek, a total of 10 million cubic metres
of wood is obtained in Ghana every year. This figure is
assumed by the present author to represent the total
quantity of wood cut or burned from the forest by all
methods. Of this total, Addo[2] states that in 1973, 2.075
million m^3 were won as logs by the logging companies.
Approximately half of this timber was exported, some after
sawing, and the remainder went to the sawmills and plywood
and veneer factories. It is the policy of the Government
of Ghana to restrict the export of logs and to encourage
the export of sawn timber and wood products. As a result,
the quantity of logs exported has been falling and the
quantity handled by the sawmills has been rising, although
the latter trend is slower. For the purpose of the present
paper, the 1973 data and some 1974 data is used.

In 1973, the sawmills of Ghana were said to number 70
located according to region as follows[2]:

Ashanti Region	− 36
Eastern Region	− 17
Western Region	− 8

Brong Ahafo Region .. .. - 6

Central Region .. .. .. - 3

They utilised a total of 0.85 million m^3 of logs. Plywood and veneer factories utilised a total of o.14 million m^3 of logs. It has been estimated[2] that the conversion factor in sawmilling is about 45% while that of plywood manufacture is 39% and that of veneer manufacture is 29%. Hence it can be estimated that waste from the sawmills and factories totalled some 0.56 million m^3 in 1973. This waste was in the form of off-cuts, sawdust, shavings and log cores from the veneer and plywood plants. Off-cuts are used for firewood and as a principal source of material for the charcoal burning industry. Sawdust is little used except for sealing charcoal kilns and some sawmills have a smouldering heap as a means of reducing the accumulation. It is estimated that 25,500 tons of sawdust are produced annually. At least one plywood factory in Kumasi has introduced a wood-fired boiler which burns a proportion of sawdust with wood off-cuts and this trend can be expected to increase.

In addition to the sawmills, there were in Ghana in 1962, (1962 Industrial Census Report Vol.1 - Industry) 1,251 wood sawing establishments. These would include traditional carpenters in informal industrial areas and a few small furniture manufacturers. Approximately, one third to one half of the timber produced by the sawmills and plywood factories is processed further by these establishments with the conversion of a proportion of the sawn timber into additional waste. Much of this waste is in the form of wood shavings produced by planing and some is used for mattress filling and some for land reclamation. Allowing a conversion factor of about 80%, it can be estimated that an additional 0.04 million m^3 of waste results from the local processing of sawn timber and plywood. Hence the total wood waste from the timber industry in Ghana can be estimated to be about 0.6 million m^3.

AVAILABILITY OF WOOD WASTE AND GHANA'S ENERGY NEEDS

The quantity of wood waste produced by the timber industry of Ghana must be considered to be only the smaller part of the total quantity produced by logging, reforestation and farming operations. Using the available data for the years 1973 and 1973, the chart shown in Figure 1 has been derived. The data are only approximate and also change from year to year. It is quite clear that the overall picture is dominated by the 60% which is taken by informal cutting and burning. Included in this amount is about 1.5 million m^3 felled in land clearance for

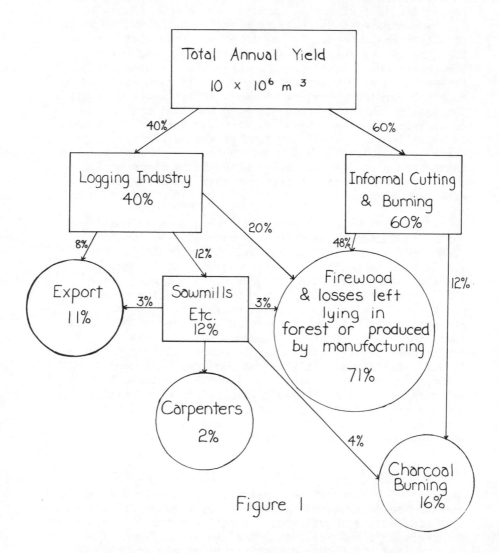

Annual Wood Flow in Ghana

Figure 1

reforestation. Ofei[4] estimates that logging operations leave behind in the forest as much felled timber as they take out. This accounts for about 20% of the annual yield. The wood waste available to provide energy as firewood and charcoal represents a very large resource. The quantity of wood involved could total some 8.7 million m^3 according to the available data. Assuming after Siwek that 80% of the Ghanaian species are suitable for use as fuel, the actual quantity of wood available to produce energy might be as low as 7 million m^3 if one allows that non-fuel species are cut down when land is cleared for farming, logging and reforestation. The heat of combustion of this quantity of wood amounts to about 10^{14} KJ. Burning steadily throughout the year, this combustion is equivalent to an energy flow of 3500 MW.

The hydro-electric power station at Akosombo on the Volta River has an installed capacity of 912 MW and represents some 95% of Ghana's electricity generating capacity. The total installed capacity in the Country is therefore less than 1000 MW. However, the power consumed by Ghana's population of 10 million is very much less than this, because the Akosombo plant does not operate at full capacity, 30-40% of its output is exported to the American Volta Aluminion Company smelter at Tema and more power is exported to Togo and Dahomey. The Volta River Authority supplied 3.9×10^9 kwh in 1975 which is equivalent to a mean power consumption of 445 MW.

It has been stated[7] that in 1973, Ghana consumed energy amounting to 4.3×10^{13} KJ. About 70% of the total was imported in the form of fuel oils and some coal. These data therefore suggest that the power consumed in Ghana is equivalent to 1500 MW of which only some 450 MW originate in Ghana. It seems probable that the latter takes no account of firewood utilisation and considers only hydro-electric power. What is more clear is that the potential power output of the wood wastes of Ghana is well in excess of the total national power consumption and about seven times the domestic electricity consumption.

No reliable estimate has yet been made of the total utilisation of wood waste for energy production in Ghana. Some estimates have been made of the size of the charcoal burning industry but these vary widely from 70,000 tons to 300,000 tons per annum. The most likely figure seems to be about 100,000 tons which is the conclusion drawn by the Capital Investment Board of Ghana. More than 99% of this total is made in traditional earth kilns with a conversion factor of from 5 to 15%. Taking a mid value of 10% gives an annual utilisation of about 1.6 million m^3 of wood waste for the charcoal burning industry. About a quarter of this total may come from the sawmills. Referring again to Figure 1 suggests that the balance of 7.1 million m^3 is used as firewood or is lost. All investigators observe that a large proportion of timber is left to rot where it falls. Losses include the branches of trees felled for logging, secondary species felled and left lying in reforested areas and large trees left lying on cleared farm land. Much timber remains unused because it is too large to be cut into pieces for head loading from the forest to the village. However, in savanna areas, where wood is scarce and trees are smaller, all of the felled timber is used and most is consumed as firewood.

PRESENT USES OF FIREWOOD AND CHARCOAL

The greatest proportion of firewood and almost all the charcoal is burned to provide heat for domestic purposes, mainly cooking. It is easy to form the impression in the town that every home has a charcoal stove. The two largest towns, Accra and Kumasi, consume about 70% of total charcoal production. However in the rural areas, large numbers of women and children are seen cutting and carrying wood to their homes. No doubt the cost of charcoal (¢7.50 = $6.52 per sack of 72lbs.) is too high for most families. It is apparent that in the Country as a whole, most families use firewood for cooking. The firewood is burned in a small mud stove of traditional design (Bokyea). A few families have metal stoves, others use old car wheels, concrete blocks or large stones to support the cooking pots. Most of the firewood is collected from the bush and costs nothing in cash terms. The women and children who do this work would not be able to spend the time to earn a cash income and so their time is regarded as free. Near sawmills, wood waste may be obtained for a small charge.

If it is assumed that 1 million Ghanaians use charcoal for cooking in the main towns of Accra, Kumasi, Takoradi, etc. and that the other 9 million use firewood to produce an equal energy supply per capita, then the firewood used for cooking in Ghana would amount to about 2.7 million m^3 or 27% of the total annual yield. Experience suggests that the industrial uses of firewood are unlikely to total more than half the domestic consumption. Hence one arrives at a very approximate total firewood utilisation of 4.0 million m^3. This represents a little over a half of the wood available and although the remainder includes some

species not suitable for firewood, it is clear that a great
abundance remains unused. This conclusion accords with the
observation made by several investigators that the logging
and reforestation operations leave large quantities of wood
to rot in the forest. It is also consistent with the fact
that firewood is considered to be a free commodity in the
forest zone; this being a sure indication that the supply
exceeds the demand by a substantial margin.

Most rural industries use firewood as their main
source of energy. The wood is burned in furnaces and open
fires of varying degrees of efficiency. As examples, one
can consider the industries making soap, glass beads, brass
castings and hand printed cloth (Adinkra). The soap boiling
tank is made of steel and has a capacity of ½ ton of soap.
It stands on a metal frame around which a stove is made from
bricks and mud. A short section of drain pipe serves as a
vent for the smoke. At the Soap Pilot Plant at Kwamo,
Ashanti, established by the Technology Consultancy Centre,
both electrically heated and firewood plants were assessed.
The fuel cost for firewood was less than one half of the
cost of electricity. The firewood plant was cheaper to
make and easier to operate. There was no doubt that the
firewood plant was the appropriate technology even in areas
where electrical power was available. In most rural areas,
there is no choice of fuel at the present time.

The furnaces for glass bead making at Dabaar, Ashanti
and elsewhere are made of brick and clay and use lorry or
car front axles for the grid which supports the clay moulds.
The furnace operates at 700–750°C. The furnaces used for
the lost wax brass casting industry at Kurofofrom, Ashanti
are made of similar materials but they are smaller, use a
hand operated bellows and operate at a higher temperature.
The design has been adversely criticised and is probably
inefficient. The Adinkra cloth printers of Ntonso, Ashanti
boil their dye over an open fire in the form of a trough
formed by large stones or concrete blocks.

Many rural industries making foods and drinks use
firewood for heating. Some examples are bread baking, fish
smoking, gari making from cassava, pito (beer) brewing and
akpeteshi (gin) brewing.

Blacksmiths generally use palm kernel charcoal for
their hearths. It is an excellent fuel for this purpose
and has replaced the use of imported coke at the Technology
Consultancy Centre Workshop.

SOME DEVELOPMENTS IN THE USE OF WOOD WASTE

The University of Science & Technology has become involved in some attempts to increase the utilisation of wood waste. In particular, the prospect of using the large quantities of sawdust from the sawmills presents a great challenge. Mr. R. S. Nijjhar of the Department of Mechanical Engineering has devised a domestic stove that burns sawdust. It appears to be successful and has created some interest locally. Attempts have been made to use the sawdust stove as a heat source for other applications. The development of a superheated-steam bread-baking oven has made some progress. An attempt to link the sawdust stove to a fan driven dryer for agricultural produce failed because the smoke tainted the product.

An application in which smoke is intended to affect the taste of the product is fish smoking. An improved fish smoking oven has been designed by Dr. B. A. Ntim of the Technology Consultancy Centre. Trials have been successfully completed at Kumasi and several ovens are now being constructed at Elmina on the coast of the Gulf of Guinea. The project is being undertaken for the Food Research Institute of the Council for Scientific & Industrial Research.

The soap boiling tank with firewood heating developed by the T.C.C. has already been described. It was designed with help from Mr. G. Prakash a Consultant from India who visited Kumasi for 3 months in 1975.

DEVELOPMENTS IN THE CHARCOAL BURNING INDUSTRY

Charcoal is made almost exclusively in the traditional earth kiln. The wood is piled and thoroughly ignited. When judged to be sufficiently hot, the pile is covered with leaves or sod and then with soil to exclude practically all air but leaving openings for the escape of smoke and controlled ventillation. When in the judgement of the charcoal burner the charring is complete, all openings are tightly closed and the pile is allowed to cool. By this method, some of the wood is burned to produce the heat required to produce the carbonisation. The yield is poor and the charcoal contains quantities of earth and ash.

Some charcoal burners have established themselves beside sawmills and use exclusively the waste timber for the pile and sawdust for the covering. This system makes use of all the waste and works to the advantage of the

sawmill in that it is relieved of the need to burn its
sawdust.

According to Siwek, the traditional charcoal kilns
used in Ghana have an efficient of conversion of only 5 to
15% whereas efficient carbonisation should provide yields
of around 25%. It is clear therefore that the annual
production using the same quantity of raw material could
increase from say, 100,000 tons to 250,000 tons if the
industry could be converted to the use of modern kilns.

The Department of Forestry has undertaken tests with
several types of kiln including the Princes Risborough
type of kiln, the Chinese kiln, Unique kiln and Tranchant
kiln. The Risborough type kiln was made from mud dried
bricks. It suffered from the disadvantage of a long
cooling time, although it achieved yields of up to 26%.
The Chinese kiln gave yields of only up to 15%. The best
results were given by the Tranchant kiln. This kiln was
made of steel and was portable. It consisted of two
cylindrical sections and a lid. Four air inlets and four
flues were arranged at the base of the bottom shell. The
average volume was about 1 cord of wood.

Welsing[5] reports some comparative tests carried out
with the Tranchant kiln and the traditional kiln. The
results are given in Table 1.

TABLE 1

AVERAGE WEIGHT OF WOOD AND CHARCOAL PER CORD RUN
(1 CORD = APPROX. 3.6 m^3 OR 128ft^3)

TYPE OF KILN	WOOD			CARBONI- SATION TIME (HOURS)	CHARCOAL YIELD		
	VOL. (CORDS)	MOISTURE CONTENT	WEIGHT OF CORD lb.		BAGS PER CORD	% GREEN WOOD	% DRY WOOD
Tranchant Kiln	1	48%	3900	50	7	12.9	19.1
Traditional Earth Mound Kiln	3.75	42%	3580	180	2.1	4.2	5.9

Other reports give the yield for the Tranchant kiln based on dry wood weight as 23% and 26%. It clearly provided a considerable advance on the traditional kiln in terms of both yield and process time.

Experiments were carried out in several places using the Tranchant kiln and people were given careful training in its use. However, the kiln has not gained acceptance and many have been abondoned. The main difficulties are the need for skilled operators and the high cost (¢800.00 in 1975) compared to traditional earth kilns which require no cash investment. This fate has befallen other attempts to introduce improved kilns. It may well be that while the availability of waste wood exceeds the demand, there is no economic incentive to seek higher efficiency. Also, Welsing reports that 98% of all workers in the charcoal burning industry received no education of any kind. Such a situation must retard the pace of technological progress. In 1975, there were reported to be only 33 modern kilns in use producing a total of 500 tons per annum[9].

The T.C.C. is hoping to collaborate with the Building & Road Research Institute (BRRI) of C.S.I.R., also located at Kumasi, to construct a pyrolytic converter developed at Georgia Institute of Technology[7]. The pyrolytic converter would be located at the B.R.R.I. brickworks at Fumesua, Ashanti and would supply fuel oil for the brick kilns as well as charcoal for local sale. The process would be continuous and the consumption of dry sawdust would be about 6 tons per day.

Siwek maintains that some species of Ghanaian timber can yield up to 30 or 40% of charcoal by weight. There is no shortage of local supplies of good quality wood, the local demand for charcoal is great and there are prospects for exporting any surplus. One estimate of the local demand for domestic use is 140,000 tons per annum. A proposed ferro-silicon plant would require a further 30,000 tons a year. In addition, Ghana imports over 600 tons per annum of activated charcoal for the sugar and pharmaceutical industries which could be produced locally by pyrolytic converters.

An excellent raw material for producing activated charcoal is coconut shell. The T.C.C. has assisted the village of Elmina to export raw coconut shells to Yugoslavia for this purpose. Together with the available waste palm kernels, another excellent raw material, waste coconut shells could be converted in Ghana into an estimated[7] 2,000 tons of activated charcoal per annum.

This operation could earn or save foreign exchange of over
$1 million every year.

Siwek expresses the view that large organisations
should be established to take up charcoal production by
modern methods. These should be situated near sawmills or
firewood plantations. However, such an approach could have
unfortunate social consequences and could lead to the demise
of the indigenous industry. This has happened to some other
industries and advocates of the intermediate technology
approach to development prefer to stimulate the gradual
upgrading of the indigenous industry. The traditional
charcoal burning industry has resisted change and it is to
be hoped that it can be persuaded to accept some technological evolution before it is swept away by the power of big
business.

GREATER UTILISATION OF WOOD WASTE

There is much evidence to suggest that the waste from
the sawmills and the informal wood-working industry is
reasonably fully utilised. Most wood waste finds its way
into the charcoal burning industry, use as firewood and
other informal industrial uses. The one area of improvement
is the utilisation of sawdust about which something has been
said. However, there is much which could be done to improve
the utilisation of the wood waste produced in the forest by
the logging operations and by land clearance for farming and
reforestation. It may be no exaggeration to suggest that 3
or 4 million m^3 of timber per annum is either burned in land
clearance or left to rot in the forest where it falls.

It is difficult to envisage a rapid change in farming
methods which would avoid burning useful timber in land
clearing operations. One can only suppose that as firewood
becomes scarcer, it will become economically necessary to
remove all useful firewood before burning the land. This
trend can already be discerned from the effects of population growth and the diminishing area of the forest. On the
other hand, much could be done to improve the utilisation of
non-commercial trees felled in land clearance and logging
operations and the branches of the trees felled for logs.
It has been estimated[4] that logging operations leave behind
40 to 50% of the wood of all trees felled. Almost no use is
made of this wood because it is too large to be cut by hand
methods, too heavy to carry by head portage and often located
in remote areas. It has been suggested that mobile sawmills
could answer this problem. The felled timber would then be
cut into manageable proportions for use as firewood or for

charcoal burning. One proposal combines the mobile sawmill
with a mobile charcoal kiln. The impediment to this type of
development would appear to be that the low value of firewood
does not allow for the cost of sawing. In the populus South
of Ghana, most firewood is regarded as free and a lorry load
of off-cuts from a sawmill costs only ₵25.00 (\$22.00) for
soft wood and ₵45.00 for hard wood. Until this situation
changes, it seems to be unlikely that any rapid development
will occur in wood waste utilisation.

It cannot be doubted that the wood waste of Ghana
represents a large reservior of energy which can be tapped
when it is needed, firstly by making use of present losses
and secondly by introducing more efficient methods of
utilisation. Perhaps the most immediate prospect lies in
the introduction of more industries using wood as fuel. It
is perhaps surprising that no wood burning steam engine is
known in the Country. The railways use steam engines burning
imported coal and, increasingly, diesel locomotives. Unlike
East Africa where wood burning steam engines were supplied
with fuel from specially prepared plantations, Ghana never
seems to have made use of its wood resources in this way.
There may be much resistance to the introduction of steam
engines for transport or industrial use at the present time.
However, the possibility may intrigue some practitioners of
intermediate technology who may find some applications where
steam power might be both technically and economically
feasible. The possibility of power generation using charcoal,.
residual oil or combustible gas from wood carbonisation or
distillation might also be explored. At a time when so much
foreign exchange is expended on petroleum products, the
incentive to produce fuels and lubricants from indigenous
raw materials is very great.

There can be little doubt that the further utilisation
of wood waste could reduce importation, support new industries and even boost exports to the great economic advantage
of the Country.

APPENDIX 1

SOME APPROXIMATE STATISTICS

Precise data are not available on many aspects of energy consumption and wood utilisation in Ghana. The following data should be taken as only very approximate. In particular, no reliable data is available on the consumption of firewood. Estimates of the quantity of charcoal produced vary by a factor of 4:1. A lower estimate is favoured as a higher one could suggest a gross utilisation of wood as charcoal and firewood in excess of the total available whereas all investigators agree that a large proportion remains unused.

Power Consumption in Ghana

Source	Mean Power Consumption (MW)
Imported oil and coal	1050
Hydro-electricity	450
Firewood (Heat of Combustion)	1035
Charcoal (Heat of Combustion)	115
TOTAL:	2650

Annual Wood Utilisation in Ghana

Use	Volume (Millions of m^3)
Export	1.1
Local Use as Timber	0.2
Charcoal Production	1.6
Firewood	4.0
Unused	3.1
TOTAL: ..	10.0

REFERENCES

1. K. SIWEK,   — 'Development of Charcoal Production
                       in Ghana', Ghana Investment Centre,
                       Investment Journal Vol.5 No.2,
                       April/June, 1974.

2. S. ADDO,   — 'Some Problems in the Utilisation of
                       the Wood Resources of Ghana'.
                       Paper No.10 — Seminar on Utilisation
                       of the Wood Resources of Ghana,
                       August, 1975.

3. J. ASMAH,   — 'Species Differentiation and
                       Manufacturing Techniques as Affecting
                       Marketing'.
                       Paper No.3 of above Seminar.

4. S. A. OFFEI,   — 'Charcoal Production and the Resources
                       in Ghana'.
                       Paper No.12 of above Seminar.

5. A. WELSING,   — 'Planning for Charcoal Burners in
                       Kumasi'. Thesis in part Fulfilment of
                       Requirements for B.Sc. in Urban
                       Planning, Faculty of Architecture,
                       U.S.T., Kumasi.

6.   — A Report on Charcoal Production in
                       Ghana by the Capital Investment Board
                       (C.I.B.), Accra, November, 1973.

7. T. I. CHIANG,
    J. W. TATOM,
    J. W. S. de GRAFT-JOHNSON,
    J. W. POWELL   — 'Pyrolytic Conversion of Agricultural
                       and Forests Wastes in Ghana — A
                       Feasibility Study' Report prepared for
                       U.S.A.I.D. by the Economic Development
                       Laboratory of Georgia Institute of
                       Technology.

8

Methane from Human, Animal and Agricultural Wastes

Raymond C. Loehr

Introduction

In considering alternatives to meet the energy needs in developing countries, there are several key items that should be recognized and achieved. These are: a) in general current methods of producing energy for domestic use, such as burning of cattle dung, crop residues, and wood, are inefficient; b) less plant fuels should be used for combustion to avoid denuding of forests and to maintain soil tilth; c) there should be higher agricultural yields; d) human drudgery should be reduced; e) the energy that is produced should be storable, and f) capital and operating expense should be minimum. In addition, the technologies that are used should be environmentally sound and adapted to and compatible with the local economic, social, and political situation. The most appropriate technology would serve the dual purpose of resource conservation and environmental protection.

Although there is no "ideal" technology that can meet all of the above goals, methane generation is a waste management technology that comes close to achieving many of the goals. The utilization of human, animal and agricultural wastes for methane generation has many positive aspects, including: a) the production of an energy resource that can be stored and is independent of fossil fuel supplies; b) the creation of a stabilized residue (sludge) that retains the fertilizer value of the original material; and c) the saving of the amount of energy required to produce an equivalent amount of nitrogen-containing fertilizer by synthetic processes. Other positive but indirect benefits of methane generation include public health such as a reduction of human pathogens if human wastes are used and a decrease of plant pathogens that may be associated with the crop residues. By using human, animal, and agricultural wastes for methane generation, the additional value of the methane can be gained while realizing other benefits. The original nutrients in the digested material can be returned to the soil as a fertilizer and to improve soil structure and organic matter content.

In many countries in which methane is produced for domestic or farm use, the drudgery of collecting wood, dried dung, or crop residues and the smoke of burning these materials has been reduced. In addition, when applied to fields, the stabilized wastes resulting from the methane generation have helped increase agricultural yields, control erosion, and maintain desirable soil characteristics.

Background

The interest in non-fossil fuel energy supplies has focused increasing attention on the production of methane from the anaerobic fermentation or digestion of organic matter such as wastes since methane is a high energy by-product. The production of methane from wastes is centuries old and the general technology is well known. The largest application of methane generation has been with municipal sewage sludge. Anaerobic digestion has been widely applied in municipal and industrial wastewater treatment plants for biologically stabilizing organic solids, reducing sludge volumes requiring ultimate disposal, odor control and re-covery of the resultant methane for plant heating and energy requirements.

In countries with low natural energy supplies and/or where there is concern over the loss of fertilizer value by alternative uses of agricultural wastes such as burning, methane has been generated from available wastes to meet the existing needs. Extensive work on methane generation has occurred in many countries, especially India, Taiwan, the United States, and Europe and several extensive reports have been published describing design, construction, operation, and results (1-5).

Individual family methane generating units have been used in diverse climatic and cultural conditions. Several thousand units are operative in Taiwan using primarily pig manure and by-products from individually owned and operated pig farms. Crop residues and cow dung have been used in family and village operated units in India for decades. Over 30,000 small methane generation units have been installed in India using some 66.9 million tons of manure which otherwise would be burned. During 1974-75 alone, some 10,000 new methane plants were installed with a goal of 100,000 being installed by 1980 (6). Units also are reported to be operating in Korea, the Peoples Republic of China, Uganda and in other countries of Asia and Africa.

All organic wastes can be fermented to produce methane. Examples of animal and agricultural wastes that can be used to produce methane are noted in Table 1. Those that have been studied or utilized most extensively are animal wastes, slaughterhouse wastes, and wastes from certain food processing industries. Much more information is available on the digestion of manure and human wastes than on crop residues.

Factors Affecting Methane Production

Biodegradability. The quantity and composition of the gases produced during anaerobic digestion are a function of the fraction of the total waste that is available to the anaerobic bacteria, i.e., the biodegradable fraction, and the operating environmental conditions of the process. The more biodegradable the waste material, the greater the quantity of methane generated per quantity of waste added to a digester. Table 2 indicates the estimated gas production from the manure of various animals produced under conditions in the United States.

As much as 8 to 9 ft^3 of gas (containing 60 to 70% methane) can be produced per pound of volatile solids added to the digester (0.5 to 0.6 m^3/kg) when the organic matter is highly biodegradable such as untreated human wastes or fresh manure. Not all wastes are equally biodegradable and effective in producing methane. The biodegradable fraction of a waste will vary being a factor of the characteristics of the material, the food ingested to generate the human or animal wastes, and how the wastes were handled prior to digestion. For example, only 40 to 50% of the volatile solids of dairy cattle manure may be biodegradable and thus available to produce methane. To use anaerobic digestion effectively, the inclusion of inert material such as sand and dirt in wastes should be minimized and wastes as fresh as possible should be utilized. When a waste is exposed to the natural environment, such as by lying on the ground, natural degradation of the organic fraction takes place and the biodegradable fraction will decrease. In addition, significant losses of nitrogen will occur.

The data in Table 2 incorporate average values obtained from the literature for manure production and biodegradability. The highest amount of gas produced per 1000 pounds live weight was from chickens, indicating the higher amount of biodegradable organics in that material. Under U.S.

Table 1. Agricultural residues having potential for methane generation

---

- Animal wastes including bedding, wasted feed, poultry litter, and manure

- Crop wastes: sugar cane trash, weeds, crop stubble, straw, and spoiled fodder

- Slaughterhouse wastes, animal by-products such as blood, meat, fishery wastes, leather, and wool wastes

- By-products of agricultural based industries such as oil cakes, wastes from fruit and vegetable processing, bagasse and press-mud from sugar factories, sawdust, tobacco wastes and seeds, rice bran, tea waste, and cotton dust from textile industries

- Forest litter

- Wastes from aquatic growths such as marine algae, sea weeds, and water hyacinths

---

Table 2. Estimated manure and bio-gas production from animal wastes (7)

	Dairy Cattle	Beef Cattle	Swine	Poultry
Manure production (lb/day/1000 lb live weight)	85	58	50	59
Volatile solids (lb dry solids/day/1000 lb live weight)	8.7	5.9	5.9	12.8
Digestion efficiency of the manure solids (%)	35	50	55	65
Bio-gas production (ft^3/lb VS added)	4.7	6.7	7.3	8.6
(ft^3/1000 lb live weight/day)	40.8	39.5	43.1	110.9

(lb x 0.454 = kg: ft^3/lb x 0.062 = m^3/kg)

conditions, the minimum animals to produce the energy equivalent to one liter of gasoline is approximately: 2 beef
cattle, 3.2 dairy cattle, 330 chickens, and 16 swine. These
values and those in Table 2 depend on the weight and feed
ration of the animals and will vary over a wide range. The
data in Table 2 estimates the gross energy possible from
digestion and does not include energy required to operate the
process.

The ratio of carbon to nitrogen (C:N) in the raw materials is important for the production of methane. Nitrogen
is needed for the synthesis and activity of the microorganisms in the anaerobic process. If there is insufficient
nitrogen to allow the anaerobic bacteria to reproduce, carbon
dioxide will be the principal gas produced. For optimum
methane production, the C:N ratio should be below about 30-35.

When largely cellulosic material is being contemplated
for methane generation, such sawdust or crop residues, nitrogen in the form of urine, nitrogen rich manures, or urea may
have to be added to have the C:N ratio in the feasible range
for best methane production.

If the waste material contains quantities of nitrogen
such that not all of the nitrogen will be used for synthesis
of the anaerobic microorganisms, the ammonia concentration
will increase. If excessive nitrogen is contained in the
wastes, the ammonia concentration may reach levels that are
inhibitory to the organisms and gas production will slow or
even cease. Should such conditions occur, the ammonia concentration should be reduced by removing portions of the digester contents, adding water to dilute the remaining
ammonia concentrations and adding carbonaceous materials to
the feed materials to restore the C:N balance. Types of
wastes that have a high nitrogen content are fish scraps,
blood, and fresh poultry manure.

It should be realized, however, that if organic material
has little biodegradable content and is resistant to microbial action, it wll not be digested even if it has a favorable C:N ratio. In summary, wastes from similar sources may
yield quite different quantities of gas. In interpreting the
feasibility of waste materials for methane production, both
the C:N ratio and the relative ease of degradation of the
material needs to be known. Caution is advised in examining
results or data obtained from systems using residues having
characteristics different from those under consideration.
The biodegradable fraction may be different and the residues
may have components that may cause inhibition of the digestion process. When wastes for which there is no specific

data are being considered for methane generation, investigations should be made to determine the operating conditions that are needed and the gas generation that will result. Knowledge of the gas production per unit of wastes added to a digester is important to the entire feasibility of methane generation since it determines the quantity of gas available for utilization and the required size of the system.

Microbial Reactions. The oxidation of organic carbon-containing compounds represents the mechanism by which heterotrophic organisms obtain the energy for their activity and for the synthesis of new organisms. In aerobic treatment systems organic carbon is transformed, via many steps to synthesized microbial protoplasm, $C_5H_7O_2N$, and carbon dioxide.

$$\text{Organic carbon} + O_2 \rightarrow C_5H_7O_2N + CO_2 \tag{1}$$

The uptake of oxygen and formation of carbon dioxide represent the effects of respiration.

In anaerobic systems, molecular oxygen is not the terminal electron acceptor and all of the respired carbon will not be transformed to carbon dioxide. Under anaerobic conditions, organic carbon is converted to microbial solids, carbon dioxide, methane, and other reduced compounds. Anaerobic metabolism leading to the formation of methane occurs in a series of steps. For simplicity these can be summarized as the conversion of complex organics to simpler compounds:

$$\text{Organic carbon} \rightarrow \text{microbial cells} +$$
$$\text{organic acids, aldehydes, alcohols, etc.} \tag{2}$$

and the conversion of the simpler compounds to gaseous end products:

$$\text{Organic acids} + \text{oxidized organic carbon} \rightarrow$$
$$\text{microbial cells} + \text{methane} + \text{carbon dioxide} \tag{3}$$

Little stabilization of organic matter occurs in the first step. Stabilization of the organic matter occurs in the second step in which the carbon compounds, carbon dioxide (CO_2) and methane (CH_4), are released to the atmosphere and removed from the substrate. The oxygen demand of the waste is thus reduced. At standard conditions, the production of 5.6 ft^3 of methane results in the stabilization of 1 lb of ultimate oxygen demand. Methane generation is a process that results in the stabilization of the wastes, i.e., reduces the biodegradability of the residual material.

These reactions must occur simultaneously since if the reactions become seriously unbalanced, the process can fail. The organic acids, generally referred to as volatile acids, produced during the first stage of the fermentation process tend to depress the pH. This effect is counteracted by the destruction of volatile acids and reformation of bicarbonate buffer during the second stage. If volatile acids build up in the system, the buffer capacity may be overcome and a precipitous drop in pH may occur. Buffering with an inexpensive base such as lime may be necessary to return the system to equilibrium. Other bases can be used but care must be exercised to avoid chemicals that may result in other inhibitory conditions.

The bacteria in the anaerobic systems are sensitive to changes in pH. The optimal pH range for methane production is between 7.0 and 7.2, and gas production is satisfactory between 6.6 and 7.6. When the pH drops below 6.6 there is a significant inhibition of the methanogenic bacteria, and acid conditions below a pH of 6.2 are toxic to these bacteria. Under balanced digestion conditions, the biochemical reactions tend to automatically maintain the pH in the proper range.

Methane bacteria are sensitive to other environmental factors. Because they are obligate anaerobes, their growth is inhibited by small amounts of oxygen and it is essential that a highly reducing environment be maintained to promote their growth. Not only oxygen, but any highly oxidized material, such as nitrites or nitrates, can inhibit the methanogenic bacteria. If chemical additives are required to help balance a digester or provide nutrients, they should be added in the most reduced forms.

The concentrations of any additives should be maintained below concentrations that may be inhibitory. A number of chemicals have been shown to be toxic to the anaerobic bacteria. The toxicity can result in a reduction of gas production, an increase in volatile acid concentration or both. Examples of inhibitory compounds are: ammonium ion (>3000 mg/ℓ) of total ammonia nitrogen at any pH; soluble sulfites (>50-200 mg/ℓ); and soluble salts of metals such as copper, zinc, and nickel. Alkaline earth-metal salts, such as those of sodium, potassium, calcium, or magnesium, may be either stimulatory or inhibitory, depending on the concentration.

With the exception of possibly ammonia, the above inhibitory materials are not likely to cause problems with "typical" human, animal, and agricultural wastes. Such wastes rarely contain the above compounds in amounts likely to be inhibitory.

One exception might be when the human wastes are combined with municipal wastes that include wastes from industry. Certain industrial wastes can add chemicals in amounts that can be inhibitory to anaerobic digestion.

Because methane production is a microbiological process, the factors affecting the process must be understood in both the selection of the material for the process and in its operation. Conditions that inhibit the process must be avoided.

Time and Temperature. The microbial reactions require time to be completed. Time is needed to degrade and solubilize the complex organic compounds in the waste and convert the soluble compounds into the gaseous and other end products (Equations 2 and 3). This time is related to the rate at which microorganisms metabolize the wastes and that rate, in turn, is a function of the temperature of the system. Thus time and temperature are interrelated.

The measure of time usually used for design or operation of biological waste treatment systems, including anaerobic digestion, is the solids retention time (SRT) sometimes referred to as MCRT (mean cell residence time) or θ_c by various authors. SRT is the time that the microbial mass is retained in the biological system.

Fundamentally, SRT should be determined using the quantity of active microorganisms in the system. However, measuring the active microbial mass in biological treatment systems is difficult. Fortunately, other parameters can be used. Assuming that there is a uniform distribution of the active microorganisms and other solids in the methane unit, SRT can be determined by using the quantity of other solids in the system, i.e., volatile suspended solids, total suspended solids, or total solids. In practice, the SRT of the system can be determined by:

$$SRT = \frac{\text{weight of solids in the system}}{\text{weight of solids leaving the system/time}} \quad (4)$$

The actual SRT of a biological treatment system must be greater than the minimum time it takes for the microorgansims to reproduce in the system. If this does not occur, the microorganisms will be removed from the system at a faster rate than they can multiply and failure of the system will result. Minimum SRT values for anaerobic systems have been estimated to be in the range of two to six days.

The temperature of the anaerobic digester will affect its performance since it affects the activity of the micro-organisms. The optimum temperature of mesophilic anaerobic treatment is 30°C to 37°C. Although the time to obtain a desired degree of treatment is less with thermophilic treatment than with mesophilic treatment, thermophilic conditions have not been demonstrated as practical or economic to date.

It does not follow that anaerobic treatment must occur at optimum mesophilic temperatures. Anaerobic activity can occur if an adequate mass of active microorganisms and a sufficiently long SRT are provided for the system. At reduced temperatures, there will be less active organisms in the system. Total gas production may be reduced if the system is operated at low temperatures. An example of the relationship between SRT, temperature, and gas production that was obtained in one study is presented in Figure 1.

Only in very large digesters is it feasible to consider heating to maintain a controlled temperature at all times. Gas utilization must be planned with the expectation of smaller amounts being generated during the colder periods.

The SRT can be increased by having large enough units so that the input wastes are held long periods of time or by separating the solids from the discharged material and recycling them to the anaerobic system (9). For locations lacking skilled manpower having the knowledge needed to operate a complex anaerobic system, solids recycle is not likely to be used.

In practice, the temperature range of 25° to 35°C and a solids retention time of 10 to 15 days appears to be the most convenient and economic. Reasonably constant temperatures are important to the process. A system with a larger SRT than necessary has only increased digester size and system costs without obtaining appreciably more methane per unit of biodegradable solids.

It may be difficult, especially in colder climates and in the winter, to maintain mesophilic temperatures in the anaerobic digester. Supplemental heat can be used to maintain the necessary microbial activity. Such heat can come from the methane that is generated but will obviously reduce the amount of methane available for other purposes. The anaerobic digestion unit should be well insulated, either artificially or by constructing the unit in the ground.

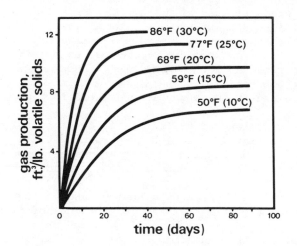

Figure 1. Bio-Gas Production as Related to the Temperature of the Digester and the Time of Digestion (7)

Sludge Utilization

The residue from a methane generation process will contain lignin, lipids, material protected from bacterial degradation, synthesized microbial cells, metabolic degradation products such as volatile acids and other soluble compounds, inert material in the original waste, and water. The residue will be a liquid with a solids concentration of 4-8 percent. Anaerobically digested sludges can be stored and spread on land with less risk of creating conditions for odor and insect breeding problems than exists with similar handling procedures for untreated or partially treated organic waste materials.

Methane generation conserves the nutrient elements needed for crop production. The only materials removed from the system, other than in the sludge, are the generated gases. Practically all of the nitrogen present in the waste entering a digester is conserved. If the sludge is properly stored, and when applied to soils is immediately incorporated to reduce the loss of nitrogen by volatilization, most of the nitrogen present in plant residues can be available for use by the growing plants. To minimize ammonia nitrogen losses, the digested sludge should be stored in lagoons or tanks which present a minimum of surface area for ammonia evaporation. Other chemical elements contained in the added waste will be conserved in the digested sludge.

The end result of applying digested sludge on soils is the same as that resulting from the application of any other kind of organic matter. The humus materials can improve soil physical properties such as aeration, moisture holding capacity, increase cation exchange capacity, and improve water infiltration capacity. The sludge can serve as a source of nutrients for crops grown on the soil. When human, animal, and agricultural wastes are used for methane generation, there is little likelihood that any items in the sludge will cause adverse conditions to the crops or to animals fed the crops grown on land where digested sludge is used as a fertilizer.

The application of the digested sludge to the crop land should be done in an environmentally sound manner, generally at rates consistent with the need of the crops being grown. Runoff that can contaminate surface waters and loadings that result in ground water contamination must be avoided.

An important aspect to be considered with methane generation is that the total volume of sludge that must be handled for final disposal is equal to or greater than the initial

amount of dry wastes that are to be digested because of the
liquid added to obtain a solids concentration that can be
mixed. Although considerable solids decomposition occurs in
a digester, approximately 50%, little reduction of the total
volume to be handled results.

Gas Utilization

Key items in the successful operation of a methane generation system are: (a) acceptance by the potential user, (b)
ability to use the gas when produced, (c) sufficient demand
for the gas, (d) enough raw material available to meet the
production requirements, and (e) suitable maintenance and
operational control.

Pure methane is a colorless and odorless gas which
generally constitutes between 60 and 70% of the gas produced
by anaerobic digestion. The other constituents are primarily
carbon dioxide and smaller concentrations of other gases
such as hydrogen sulfide and hydrogen. Digester gas
(biogas) burns with a blue flame and has a heat value ranging
about 600 to 700 Btu/ft^3 (22,000 to 26,000 kj/m^3) when
its methane content ranges from 60 to 70 percent.

Many options exist for utilizing the digester gas. It
can be used directly in gas-burning appliances for heating,
cooking, lighting and refigeration or it can be used as fuel
for internal combustion engines having a compression ratio of
8:1 or greater. However, to use digester gas in internal
combustion engines, it is necessary to a) reduce the hydrogen
sulfide content of the gas to less than 0.25 percent to prevent corrosion of metal surfaces, b) provide a system to
remove the carbon dioxide to increase the heat content per
unit volume of the resultant gas, c) compress the gas to a
volume that would fit on a vehicle or adjacent to a stationary
engine, and d) have an internal combustion engine converted
to use either gasoline or methane.

Another possible use is the production of electricity
using methane. However, the cost of converting the methane
to electricity currently results in an energy cost that is
higher than that available from other sources. As the cost
of more traditional energy sources increases, the costs of
electricity production from methane may become more attractive.

For small units, it is not practical to compress and
store the gas for subsequent use. Major use of such gas must
be at the production site. The gas is generally and most
simply used for heat or light in appliances that use the gas
directly from low-pressure collection units. A small digester

with a floating cover can provide the needed gas storage.
Another approach is to have gas from a digester with a fixed
cover piped for collection in an auxiliary gas holder with a
floating cover. A gas delivery line is connected to the gas
storage unit with an on-off control valve. This delivery
line must contain a flame trap installed between the gas
storage unit and the appliance being used. Systems of this
type are in current use in India, Taiwan and other warm
climate areas.

The size of the digester and gas collection unit is
related to the rate of gas that is utilized and the number
of appliances that are connected. Consumption rates for gas
burning appliances (Table 3) are useful in determining the
necessary sizes.

Although general information on the design of anaerobic
digesters is available, the state-of-the-art of anaerobic
digestion of agricultural wastes is not such that all producers can successfully operate an anaerobic digester nor
utilize the resultant gas. Considerable investigation and
full scale testing in specific situations may be needed to
show the practicality and feasibility of energy recovery from
the anaerobic digestion of the available human, animal, and
agricultural wastes.

Collection and Preparation

An important aspect of methane generation is the collection and preparation of the materials to be used in the process. When considering the feasibility of a methane production system, all of the components, i.e., collection,
preparation, storage of the raw material, generation, storage
of the gas and residue, and utilization of the gas and residue
must be considered. Capital and labor requirements and annual
costs must be determined for all the components and related
to the local labor, material, and cost conditions.

In labor-intensive economies, methods that can utilize
the human and animal resources available for the handling and
processing of these wastes should be considered. Since the
intent of anaerobic digestion is to produce an energy source,
methods that utilize fossil fuel or other conventional sources
of energy for handling, processing, heating and mixing these
wastes may not be appropriate unless there is a significant
net benefit.

The collection and processing of raw waste materials
depends on their nature, which may vary between countries and
regions, as well as the quantities in which they are available.

Table 3. Quantities of bio-gas required for a specific application (10)

Use	Specification	Quantity of Gas Required ft^3/hr	m^3/hr
Cooking	2" burner	11.5	0.33
	4" burner	16.5	0.47
	6" burner	22.5	0.64
Gas lighting	per mantle	2.5-3.0	0.07-0.08
	2 mantle lamp	5	0.14
	3 mantle lamp	6	0.17
Gasoline or diesel engine [a]	Converted to bio-gas	16-18 per hp	0.45-0.51 per hp
Refrigerator	per ft^3 capacity	1	0.028
Incubator	per ft^3 capacity	0.45-0.6	0.013-0.017
Gasoline	1 liter	47-66 [b]	0.013-0.017
Diesel fuel	1 liter	53-73 [b]	1.50-2.07 [b]
Boiling water	1 liter	2.2 [c]	0.62 [c]

[a] Based on 25 percent efficiency

[b] Absolute volume of bio-gas needed to provide energy equivalent of 1 liter of fuel

[c] Absolute volume of bio-gas needed to heat 1 liter of water to boiling

Hence the method for collecting and handling the waste
materials may vary. The materials available for methane
generation may be solid, semi-solid or liquid. Thus the
collection methods that will be needed will be related to
the characteristics of the wastes and the socially acceptable
methods of handling them.

Crop residues such as spent straw, hay, sugar cane trash,
plant stubble, grasses, and bagasse can be used for the generation of methane. To enhance gas production, facilitate
their mixing and transport in and out of the digester, and to
avoid clogging, such material should be finely chopped or
shredded. In rural areas manually operated shredders could
be used.

When different wastes are to be added, they should be
mixed prior to their addition to the digester. The wastes
should be added daily to the digester to insure a continuous
supply of gas and to avoid a deterioration of the methane
generation process. Accumulated wastes can be stored briefly
before being added to the digseter. Care should be taken to
avoid losses of nutrients, fly breeding, or odors during the
storage.

Equipment

The main components of a methane generation system are
a raw waste feeding unit, a digestion unit, a gas holder, a
moisture trap, and an outlet for the gas to be utilized and
the digested solids. A sketch of a small scale system for
heating and lighting use is shown in Figure 2. For larger
systems and other uses, a methane generation system may include a raw waste storage unit and units for hydrogen sulfide
and carbon dioxide removal and gas compression.

The pieces of equipment can be made from many types of
material. Where available, brick, cement, concrete, and
steel pipe can be used. The gas holder may be a steel drum.
Lime mortar can be used if cement is in short supply. Other
material such as glazed pottery rings cemented together and
similar local materials can be used to construct the needed
equipment. Hand plungers can be used to force the feed
material into the digester. Both horizontal and vertical
digesters have been used with vertical units being predominant
in countries where biogas plants are in operation. For small
systems and needs, large inner tubes have been used as gas
collectors. The simplest system consistent with the need and
labor available should be constructed. Materials that are
long lasting and require minimum maintenance should be used.

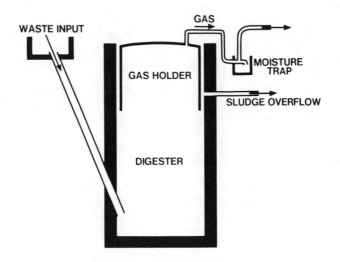

Figure 2.   Schematic of a Small Scale Bio-Gas Digester

When the raw wastes are added to the digester, the digested slurry automatically overflows and should be captured for subsequent use as a fertilizer. The slurry can overflow into a container filled with straw, leaves or similar material and used as a solid or semi-solid fertilizer. It can also be collected as a liquid and used in that form.

Operation

In a developing country and a rural setting it is unlikely that a continuous anaerobic digester would be used, because of the necessary feeding and controlling mechanisms. A batch or semi-continuous operation is the more common method of operation. A digester may operate on a "fill and draw" basis with a one-day to one-week cycle, or it may be designed on an "all-in, all-out" basis where the reactor is charged and emptied when gas production is almost completed or at a very low level. A combination of the two systems also may be considered depending upon particular needs. The semi-continuous digesters are used for waste that is available on a frequent, preferably daily, basis. Most digesters in developing countries operate as semi-continuous units.

Batch-fed digesters can be constructed where raw waste materials are difficult to obtain on a daily basis. The wastes are added to the digesters, covered and permitted to digest. After an initial interval that will depend upon the temperature of the digester and whether the digester has been seeded with active anaerobic organisms, gas production will begin and continue until all the biodegradable material is used. When gas production ceases the digesters are opened, cleaned, and the slurry is disposed of on land as a fertilizer. Because of the batch nature of the system, it is desirable to have two or more digesters, so that one or more can always be in operation and gas production be fairly continuous. Periodic emptying of the digesters is labor intensive and can be unpleasant. When batch units are emptied, about one quarter of the digester contents should be left to seed the incoming raw material.

Biogas production is dependent upon the concentration of solids in the influent material. Too thick of a material will retard natural mixing in the digester and may require mechanical mixing. Investigations indicate that, in the absence of toxic materials, optimum gas production is obtained with a total solids concentration of about 7 to 10% in the effluent slurry. This may require a dilution of one part manure to two or three parts of water depending upon the initial condition of the manure.

Economics and Feasibility

Although methane generation has been successful in specific areas such as in India and Asia, economic considerations may preclude or limit its adoption in other countries. The economic feasibility of methane generation from wastes can vary widely and is dependent on factors that include the availability of domestic sources of energy, the cost of imported fuel, the uses and actual benefits from methane production, public and private costs associated with the development and utilization of methane, the availability of wastes to produce a consistent supply of methane, and on the equipment and manpower need to generate methane.

The availability and accessibility of other domestic energy sources and the opportunities to use the methane are important determinants of the feasibility of methane production. The opportunity costs associated with the use of other energy sources, such as the use of coal or petroleum for industrial expansion, need to be taken into account.

Studies in industrialized countries with access to fossil fuels indicate that methane generation is not economical even for farm and small communities with the present technology and energy costs. Methane generation is likely to have its greatest use in areas remote from fossil fuels or other energy sources, where available fuels are better used for other purposes, and for small villages and activities where the methane is used at or close to the production site.

Generally, the cost of a methane generation system and its operation has been charged against energy production. The direct benefits are those accruing from heating, cooking, lighting, refigeration, pumping irrigation water, or running other power units. However, other benefits also may accrue as a result of methane generation, such as improved public health, agricultural productivity increases, and increased employment. The use of village scale digesters can provide a sanitary means of human waste disposal that might otherwise be lacking. These benefits, although less tangible than direct energy use should be taken into account when distributing the costs of methane generation.

In addition, the wastes would have required some expense for environmentally sound management. The costs charged to methane generation should be those that are in addition to the waste handling and pollution control costs that would normally occur.

In order for a methane generation program to be successful in most developing countries, some financial and continuing technical assistance from central and local governments
will be needed. Part of the material and equipment cost of
individual methane generators might be the responsibility of
central and/or local governments. Trained technical personnel
can be important to help the local people learn to install,
operate, and maintain methane digesters. The importance of
technical assistance should not be minimized. Demonstration
facilities may be required, and early adopters may need to be
subsidized as an incentive to aid the large-scale adoption of
this technology. The particular educational means to obtain
wide scale use of methane generation can vary among regions
and countries.

It is technically feasible to generate methane from
human, animal, and agricultural wastes if the factors discussed earlier are understood and properly utilized. The
economic feasibility of methane generation will depend upon
the particular set of circumstances and can only be evaluated
on an individual basis. In addition to the cost of the equipment, manpower, disposal, and opportunity costs of alternatives, of particular interest are the needs and goals of the
areas, countries, and regions, and the impact on the culture
and social fabric of the individuals and communities to be
involved.

Methane generation must be considered as part of a total
resource conservation and utilization system. Factors such
as availability of the wastes, collection, transport, methane
generation, gas and sludge use, energy needs, manpower, and
the social and cultural effect need to be considered in an
inter-related and holistic manner. Only in such a manner can
the actual feasibility of methane generation in a developing
country be ascertained.

Summary

Extensive experience with methane generation, especially
at the village or smaller level, has been obtained in several
countries and over several decades. Methane generating plants
can be designed either to process a given amount of waste
material, or to produce a given quantity of gas required for
a specific use or uses. Irrespective of which approach is
taken, an understanding of the parameters that govern the
process of anaerobic digestion is essential for proper design
and use of biogas plants.

Digester design, waste input, and gas utilization must
be tailored to the manpower and other resources, energy and

social needs, climatic conditions, and materials in each
locale. All of these factors must receive close consideration when the feasibility of a methane generation system is
evaluated. A technical assistance program may be needed in
areas where methane generation is determined to be feasible.
It is desirable to have local involvement in the planning,
construction, and operation of the digester and in the utilization of the gas and the sludge. Use of suitable local
materials and equipment should be investigated.

Before methane generation is utilized in any area or
with specific wastes, the equipment should be demonstrated to
be functional at the scale of the proposed operation, the
operation should be simple, the system should have clear,
preferably written, instructions for operation, the equipment
and its capacity should be suitable for the quantities and
types of material(s) to be handled and compatible with other
components, and users and/or operators must be capable of
properly maintaining and operating the methane generating and
utilization equipment.

Individuals who have experience with the methane generation are cautiously optimistic about its prospects. The
fundamentals of the process are well known, there is a signi-
licant quantity of human, animal, and agricultural wastes
that may be available, and these wastes can produce large
quantities of methane gas. The present technology can be
utilized and adapted to local conditons where appropriate.
Such utilization should occur only with competent guidance
and after a careful evaluation of the technical, economic,
and social feasibility.

Acknowledgements

The material that is presented is a brief summary of the
important factors affecting the use and operation of methane
generation facilities. Many comprehensive reports and
articles (1-6, 10-13) are available on the subject, some with
specific emphasis on the use of methane generation in
developing countries and rural areas. Individuals wishing
to pursue the subject in greater depth are encouraged to read
the noted articles and reports as well as others that are
available.

References and Notes

1. Tietjen, C. "From biodung to biogas - historical review of European experience." Energy, Agriculture and Waste Management, Jewell, W. Ed., Ann Arbor Science Publishers, Ann Arbor, Michigan. 247-260, 1975.

2. National Academy of Sciences, Methane Generation from Human, Animal and Agricultural Wastes, Washington, D.C. 1977.

3. Singh, R.B. Bio-Gas Plant. Generating Methane From Organic Wastes. Ajitmal, Etawah, (U.P.), India: Gobar Gas Research Station, 1971.

4. Fry, L.J. Practical Building of Methane Power Plants for Rural Energy Independence. Santa Barbara, California: Standard Printing, 1974.

5. Chung, Po. "Production and use of methane from animal wastes in Taiwan." Proceedings, International Biomass Energy Conference. Biomass Energy Institute, P.O. Box 129, Winnipeg, Manitoba, Canada. 1973.

6. Srinivasan, H.R. "Bio-gas and manure from the waste of farm animals," Khadi and Village Industries Commission, Bombay, India, January 1977.

7. Morris, G.R., Jewell, W.J., and Casler, G.L. "Alternative animal waste anaerobic fermentation designs and their costs." Energy, Agriculture and Waste Management, Jewell, W. Ed., Ann Arbor Science Publishers, Ann Arbor, Michigan. 317-336, 1975.

8. Smith, R.J. "The anaerobic digestion of livestock wastes and the prospects for methane production." Agric. Eng. Dept., Iowa State Univ., Ames, Iowa. 1973.

9. Loehr, R.C. Pollution Control for Agriculture. Academic Press, New York. 1977.

10. Singh, R.B. "The bio-gas plant: Generating methane from organic wastes." Compost Science. 20-25, Jan-Feb, 1975.

11. Patankar, G.L. "Role of gobar gas plants in agro-industries." Khadigramodyog (India), 20 (April):351-357, 1974.

12. New Alchemy Institute, Methane Digesters for Fuel, Gas, and Fertilizer. Newsletter No. 3. Woods Hale, Massachusetts, 1973.

13. Compere, A.L. and W.L. Griffith. "Anaerobic mechanisms for the degradation of cellulose." ORNL-5056, Oak Ridge National Laboratory, Oak Ridge, Tennessee, 1975.

Summary and Discussion

Roger Revelle

We had a wonderfully interesting discussion
today. In different ways nearly all of it was
about solar energy. Mr. Löf started out this
morning by talking about the direct absorption of
solar radiation and its use for heating and cooling. Mr. Prinz discussed the conversion of the
radiant energy coming from the sun into electricity
by the photovoltaic method, and the further utilization of the high temperatures generated in this
process as a source of useful heat. Mr. Tewari
talked about the uses of wind energy in India, but
of course the energy of the wind results from the
differential heating of the earth by the sun, so
it too is a form of solar energy. Mr. Ermenc
talked about small-scale hydroelectric power.
Here, the radiant energy from the sun is converted
into gravitational energy through the hydrologic
cycle, and the hydroelectric plant in turn con-
verts this gravitational energy into electrical
energy. This afternoon Mr. Sakr discussed the use
of flat plate collectors and concentrators for the
direct conversion of solar energy into heat in
Egypt, and Mr. Loehr talked about the use of biological materials as a means of converting solar
energy into humanly useful work. From an energy
point of view, as he pointed out, the non-edible
portions of agricultural crops are just as much a
potential resource as the part that can be eaten
by human beings, because energy for cooking is an
integral part of the human food system everywhere.
If we were forced to subsist on raw food, there
simply would not be enough to eat for the large

151

numbers of human beings who now live on this planet,
not to mention all the other things we do with
energy that make the difference between living like
human beings and living in an inhuman way. Then
Dr. Powell talked about another biological device
for converting solar energy--the use of wood in
Ghana and the potential for using a good deal more.
And finally Mr. Miccolis talked about the very
impressive new energy program in Brazil, in which
sugar cane and other biological converters of
solar energy will be used in an attempt to solve
their severe energy crisis. Brazil apparently has
very little oil (at least on land) and not much
usable coal, and the four or five-fold rise in the
price of imported fossil fuels is causing serious
economic problems. These same problems will be
faced by every country in about 30 years, when the
oil reserves start to run out. So the Brazilians
are simply pioneers in a situation that may become
universal within our lifetimes.

If we summarize what we have learned about all
these methods of using solar energy it is clear
that we are really concerned with the best allocation of resources, which is the central theme of
economics. One characteristic of resources is
that they are scarce. There aren't enough of them
to go around, and consequently there are always
competing uses and needs for resources. Unless we
allocate resources as economically, rationally and
prudently as possible in the face of competing
needs, the processes of development in the poor
countries will become much more difficult. The
economic objective of development can be quite
simply defined: to increase human productivity.
How can resources be best allocated to increase
human productivity, which is the only way that
real incomes can be raised? Incidentally, when we
think about appropriate technologies for the
developing countries, our criterion should be
whether these technologies are in fact likely to
increase productivity. This can be accomplished
in two ways, either by producing more per man-hour,
or by increasing the number of man-hours, i.e. by
increasing employment.

In choosing among energy sources and uses for
the rural areas of developing countries, we are
concerned with scarce resources and their most
economical allocation, both the natural resources

of land, water, fertilizer, metals, and fuels, and
the human resources of capital, labor, human energy,
skills, management and organization. The scarcest
resource of all in most developing countries is
trained management ability--the ability to organize
and administer, to create an organization and to
make it work.

We must also ask what are the needs for new
sources of energy? One need is to reduce human
drudgery, as Professor Loehr pointed out this
afternoon. Theodore Schultz, the great agricultural economist of the University of Chicago, tells
a wonderfully illustrative story. He talked to
some women in a village in Senegal, who were
threshing millet by pounding a heavy pestle into a
large wooden mortar. They had to do this all day
to separate the millet grains from the chaff. It
was very hard, very dull work. They said "We've
heard about a thresher in the next village that
does this mechanically. If we had one we wouldn't
have to do this task by hand. Why can't we have
one?" We tend to think of people in less developed
countries with high levels of unemployment and
underemployment as being eager to work in hard
drudging tasks if they have the opportunity, tasks
which will require them to use about half their
food energy in work. We think of such drudgery as
being natural for them, but we don't think of it as
being natural for us. In fact, there are probably
few human beings anywhere who are fond of continuous hard manual labor, such as the labor involved
in traditional farming.

A second need for new sources of energy is to
reduce costs. The most expensive form of energy
is human energy, as can easily be seen if we consider how much food it takes to keep a man going at
hard manual labor. Ricardo's "iron law" says that
wages always tend to go down to the subsistence
level, i.e. to the level where a working man is
able to buy with his wages barely enough food to
feed himself and his family. But the corollary to
Ricardo's law is that wages can't go below the
level of subsistence, and this level is not cheap.
It takes about 15 cents a day to feed a man even on
the least expensive of diets, and he is able to put
out somewhat less than a kilowatt hour per day of
useful work. Even at present costs of fossil fuels
a kilowatt hour from gasoline costs about 3 cents.

Animal energy is also expensive. Consider for
example the opportunity costs of feeding a bullock.
A farmer can use part of his land to grow fodder
for his bullock, but he could grow wheat or rice or
corn on that same land.

Finally, new sources of energy are needed in
order to increase the total amount of energy available. In my talk this morning, for example, I
showed that by increasing the quantity of energy
used in agriculture, the annual yields per hectare
could be tripled or quadrupled.

What are the specifications or characteristics
to be kept in mind in evaluating potential new
energy sources? To be most useful in less developed countries, any potential energy source should
have a low capital output ratio, the income
obtained each year should be at least half and
preferably equal to the capital investment. The
capital costs should be low for another reason:
capital is scarce in developing countries and cor-
respondingly interest rates are, or should be, very
high. If the capital costs for a new energy source
are a large part of the total costs high interest
rates are likely to make it uneconomical. For the
same reason it should be possible to amortize the
investment over a long lifetime, i.e. the rate of
depreciation should be low. Small unit costs are
desirable in order to keep the investment from
being "lumpy." For this reason "micro" or "mini"
hydropower plants using "run-of-the-river" installations are attractive.

Any energy source for developing countries at
the present time should be manpower-intensive
rather than capital-intensive. Its development
should use people rather than capital because
people are less expensive and more abundant than
capital in most less developed countries. In other
words, energy investments, like other investments,
should take account of the factors of production.
But one scarce kind of manpower is skilled manpower.
Hence new energy installations should be as simple
as possible, because there are so many competing
demands for skilled manpower. If possible there
should not be other competing uses for a new energy
source. For example wood can be used for industrial purposes as well as for fuel, and in mountainous regions it is essential to leave the trees

where they are to prevent erosion. Straw, if it is
not burned for energy, can be used for animal
feeding and for compost to fertilize farm fields.

In the hills of Nepal the farmers are reluctant to use the new dwarf varieties of rice because
these new varieties don't produce much straw. They
need straw to feed their livestock. They need the
livestock to produce dung to fertilize their fields.
During the monsoon season the cattle and buffalo
gather nitrogen from pasture land, and part of this
nitrogen is excreted in their dung. The farmers
collect the dung and carry it to the fields as
fertilizer. During the dry season little nutrient
material remains in the pastures, and the livestock must be fed on straw. Here is a closed
farming system which is very hard to break into or
to change. From an energy standpoint the farmers
would be unable to convert the energy in the straw
into some other form of energy because they must
feed it to their livestock.

In many cases, in less developed countries,
local energy sources should be used rather than
centralized sources, and local energy conversion
plants should be constructed rather than central
energy conversion plants. For example, the load
factors for electric power are usually quite low,
and consequently the capital costs of electric
transmission systems from central plants per unit
of energy are very high.

Problems of energy storage arise because local
energy sources are not available all the time.
Energy storage is essential if the inedible parts
of crops such as corn stalk or rice straw are to be
used as an energy source. When these inedible portions are left standing in the fields after the end
of the growing season, their contained energy
quickly disappears into the air. They must be used
when they are freshly cut. Similarly the contained
energy of sugar cane rapidly disappears after it is
harvested. If one attempts to use run-of-the-river
hydropower in Nepal or elsewhere in the Indian subcontinent, there will be a great excess of river
flow in the monsoon season (from the middle of June
to the middle of September) and very little flow
during the other eight months of the year. Some
way must be found to store the energy that is present in great abundance during the monsoon season

for use during the dry season.

Storage is one of the problems of methane production from biological materials. Methane is difficult to store because it is so light. A large
volume of storage is required, or else an expensive
high-pressure tank. This argues for making liquid
fuels such as methanol or ethanol from biological
materials, rather than gaseous fuels.

Even the direct conversion of solar energy by
photocells or by heat absorption has the problem
that sunshine varies a lot, not only between day
and night, but during the course of the year, particularly in the monsoon climates of the tropics.
During four months of the year the radiation from
the sun is obscured by heavy clouds, and considerably less radiation is received at the ground than
during the wintertime. As Mr. Sakr pointed out,
this is not true for Egypt or other desert areas,
where there are hardly ever any clouds. But the
populations of deserts are sparse, orders of mag-
nitude smaller than those of India, Pakistan,
Bangladesh, Southeast Asia and Indonesia, where the
monsoon dominates the climate.

One way to store energy is to make nitrogen
fertilizer. Even with the most efficient modern
processes for nitrogen fixation, about 15000 kilowatt hours are required to produce a ton of fixed
nitrogen. With the old electric arc process, perhaps more than 45000 kilowatt hours are required
per ton of nitrogen. With the Norwegian electrolysis process, hydropower can be used to produce
hydrogen by electrolyzing water. The hydrogen is
then used as an electron acceptor for nitrogen in
making ammonia.

Other possibilities for energy storage are
other chemical products. With present fossil fuel
costs it may actually be less expensive to make
many chemical products out of ethanol or methanol
than out of petroleum. This may not be true at
present in the United States, because we have sunk
so much capital in petrochemical plants, but thirty
years ago a good deal of technological research was
devoted to the development of methodologies for
using organic sources to make what are now called
petrochemicals.

So-called pump-back storage--pumping water up
into a high reservoir during off-peak hours, and
using this water to augment power production during
peak load periods--is another way to store energy,
at least over short periods, in order to minimize
required generator capacities.

Careful studies are needed of energy systems
in rural villages. I have mentioned the farmers in
the hills of Nepal, whose energy system is tightly
locked into their food system, with the result
that it is hard to break into either. Village
energy systems are also likely to interact with
village social systems. For example, village level
biogas plants using human wastes might be constructed to provide energy for a large fraction of
the village population. Such centralized plants
would require that the village people defecate in a
central latrine instead of the shady bamboo groves
they have been using for thousands of years. For
several reasons--some of them obvious--village
people don't like to use latrines. It may be necessary to find ways of paying them to change their
ancient habits so that the human wastes can be collected for use in a central village biogas plant.
Small family biogas plants will provide enough
energy to be useful only for those farmers who
have five or more dung-producing cattle. In this
case, the rich farmers will be better off and the
landless laborers worse off than they are at
present. The landless laborers and other dependent
people in a village now usually have a time-honored
agreement with the landowner to provide them with
straw and dung to cook with, in return for certain
traditional services. These agreements will be
broken if the landowner finds a profitable use for
the dung. This is simply one example of the fact
that the entire energy system of a village must be
carefully examined in ways that have not received
much attention from anthropologists--because anthro-
pologists are usually uninterested in economics--
to find out what actually can be done to improve
the quality of village life and particularly the
quality of life of the poorest people in the
village.

If we attempt to apply the criteria I have
outlined, it is clear that choices among different
potential energy sources will depend upon differences in environmental condition, including the

social environment. For example, wind energy may
be most useful in coastal regions, where average
wind speeds are likely to be higher than 5 meters
per second (more than 10 miles per hour). In
desert areas where there is plenty of sunshine but
little or no water, direct conversion of solar
energy, using photocells or other types of collectors, may prove to be economical, provided costs
can be sufficiently lowered, at least in areas such
as Saudi Arabia, the Persian Gulf states, or the
southwestern United States, in which investment
capital is easily available. Small-scale, "run of
the river" hydropower may be preferable in hilly
or mountainous regions with many perennial streams,
such as Nepal and the Himalayan foothill regions
of India and Pakistan. Plantations of quick-
growing trees or coarse grasses will be most
promising in regions with abundant water supply
and large areas of non-arable land, including
parts of Africa and South America. In large,
sparsely populated countries such as Brazil, where
there is an excess of well-watered, potentially
arable land, biological conversion of solar energy
by production of methanol or ethanol from sugar
cane or other high-yielding crops may be an
optimal energy source.

The most difficult problems arise in densely
populated regions with relatively small areas such
as Japan, Bangladesh, and the island of Java.
Useful supplements to existing energy sources can
be obtained in these regions from the non-edible
portions of agricultural crops, but it may be
impossible to satisfy their future energy needs
without extensive reliance on fossil fuels, and
in the long run, on nuclear energy.

Questions and Answers

Question: This morning you discussed the relationship between nondomestic consumption of energy and
productivity. Later in your talk you talked about
one way of using energy more efficiently, viz., a
better stove and a better cooking pot. So what
you are referring to at this point is domestic use
of energy. Now when domestic uses of energy become
more efficient what is going to keep people from
still channeling most energy into domestic rather
than nondomestic uses? Let me give you an example.
In many of the less developed countries people cook

their meals once a day. If they have more energy
available, why not cook twice a day? Or why not
wash their clothes in hot water? How are you going
to keep from widening the gap between domestic and
nondomestic uses of energy? In other words what
would keep people in the less developed countries
from emulating their cousins in more developed
countries by becoming more consumptuous?

Mr. Revelle: I would not object to that if the
energy were available. After all, the purpose of
life is to live as much as you can. But the problem is that these poor people don't have the
energy. As I said today, one person in a family
may spend his (or usually her) entire time just
gathering fuel. This chore is getting harder and
harder all the time as populations grow. So that
you have a tradeoff here of resources: the fuel-
gatherer will work less, gathering less fuel if he
gets a better stove. Or he may decide it's
alright to continue to work hard and cook twice a
day. He would at least have more choice than he
has right now. He has no choice at all. He is
just barely making it now.

Comment from the floor: I think basically the
problem hinges upon making the nondomestic uses of
energy and food for that matter more attractive
economically than the domestic ones. I can't help
thinking about the situation in the north of Ghana
where it is commonly understood that to increase
the food production by 20% will achieve nothing
because the people can eat 20% more food, and in
fact they are hungry for two months of the year.
They call it the hungry season. They virtually
have nothing to eat. So I think we should all
realize that we have this backlog to make up. Yes,
people are going to use more energy domestically,
yes they are going to eat more food domestically,
but let's give them the chance to make that for-
ward step first. Then we must think about ways of
using their time, their energy and their resources
for economic activities which will be to their own
personal benefit. And then they will choose for
themselves how they use their resources and their
energy.

Question: Can any of the panel members identify
strategies for development of energy and other
resources which are more likely to encourage

demographic transition or whatever you choose to
call it, such that the proceeds won't tend to be ·
eaten up?

Mr. Revelle: I don't know that there is any
simple relationship. But I guess I should have
amplified my statement about increasing productivity by saying that it should be increased more
rapidly than populations grow. That of course is
in a sense the definition of productivity per man.
We need to remember that people have hands as well
as mouths. They can produce as well as consume.
In general, it seems to be true that if the
poorest people see a way in which their lives can
be improved and in which their children's lives
can be improved, they are very likely not to have
so many children. That seems to be the experience
of many countries where this kind of improvement
has taken place.

Question: For example on the Indian subcontinent?

Mr. Revelle: Oh yes. For example in Sri Lanka,
where there is a fairly good income distribution
compared to the rest of the subcontinent--every-
body in Sri Lanka receives a free kilogram of rice
once a week and pays only 2 annas for another kg;
every village has a dispensary, every market town
has a clinic, every little city has a hospital,
all free for everyone in the country; education up
to and including the university is free, and there
are about as many educated women as men. And Sri
Lanka has the lowest birthrate in the subcontinent.
Taiwan, Korea, Singapore, Hongkong, Malaysia,
particularly West Malaysia, Costa Rica, countries
where there is a relatively good income distribution, where living conditions of the poor have
been and are improving, all have low birth rates.
Improving the living conditions of the poor may be
a necessary if not a sufficient condition for
reducing population growth. This improvement may
well depend on obtaining and distributing more
energy.

Index